Amassing Power

A History of Oppressive Systems since 1850

By Ralph Brandt

Updated July 2020 in the middle of the COVID situation and the unrest by the radical left.

third Edition 2020

Copyright 2017, 2018, 2019,2020

Table of Contents

Dedication: This book is dedicated to the memory of my parents, Ralph Roscoe Brandt and Rachel Irene Brandt (Bupp). They instilled in me a faith in God, a love for my fellow man, a respect for my country and a desire to learn. Neither finished high school. My dad quit late in his senior year (1930) because the family did not have the money for him to graduate. He went on to learn in other forums and finished his career as an Assistant Plant Manager for Duffy Mott Company. He became a respected expert in electrical systems, food canning machinery, and food canning processes. My mom left school in eighth grade and was hired out as an indentured servant to help the family finances in 1930. Her dad promised her high school if she did that for a couple years, a promise he failed to keep. Although she never finished high school her four children did and three, June, Joan and I are college graduates with degrees in Elementary Ed., Home Making and Math, respectively. We all have post-baccalaureate work. She knew well the value of education. About two years after her death at 82 in 1997 one of my sisters mentioned that she wished we had helped her get a GED, even if it was in the last years. I regret we didn't. But informally she learned much over the years. Both read and studied extensively and had wisdom far beyond their formal education experience.

Introduction

Oppression has been with us in various forms since the beginning of time. The feudal system, the brutal governments, the Inquisition, both sides of the Crusades, Communism, Nazism, and slavery, forms of oppression have existed for eons. I show it can come from any quarter even from some seemingly benevolent governments.

This study starts as America was facing the most devastating war in its history, The [1]War of Southern Rebellion, incorrectly called the Civil War. This war ultimately ended slavery, one form of oppression, but prosecuting it brought more oppression during the war and the backwash of it opened the door for a revival of oppression, the neo-

------

[1] It was called that until the mid-1880's. The Pennsylvania Memorial at Gettysburg (about 1880), the war memorial in Penn Park York PA (about 1870) and many others call it The War of Southern Rebellion or The Recent War of the Rebellion. We have been erasing history for over 140 years.

slavery of Government oppression of blacks and whites. This war extended beyond the battle fields, past 1865, when it extended into the hearts of men and the Bible says those are intensely wicked. That wickedness reared its ugly head about 1895 and continued till well into the 20th Century with hellish practices that were in too many cases, not infractions of the law, but provided by the law itself. [2] Some of that evil continues to drive actions to this day by political groups that will use the issue of slavery to keep blacks in bondage with the handout rather than the hand up. This is an abridged study, a complete one is beyond this or any author. I believe that in pointing out the ones I have, the astute reader will be able to ferret out others.

When one looks at an oppressive power there are two aspects, the internals, how a system treats its citizens and the external, and how it treats the world around it. Some of the ones we will study did badly in one of the two and some were bad with both. Woodrow Wilson's Office of Information Commission, a virulent propaganda arm was brutal in dealing with portions of the American Citizens, particularly those of German and Austrian descent and black Americans, but on the outside, he was somewhat benign. Other than the dealing with the enemy nations he seemed to be almost sweetness and light. He was in fact, one of the earliest globalists. His League of Nations is lauded today by many left-leaning college professors and they blame World War II on the failure of congress to support his efforts. I see it entirely different. I am sure things would have been different, but I believe World War II was inevitable unless the national leaders in Germany, Italy and most important, Japan were toppled. Without the removal of the Emperor of Japan and the Japanese militarists from power, or the capitulation of Asia and the South Pacific to the Japanese a Pacific war on a large scale was inevitable. Sure, Hitler and Mussolini were bent on conquest, but Japan as a nation saw themselves as the super-race as much or more. I do not see the League as more effective in preventing world problems than the UN. It has failed miserably, lacking the will to confront evil men. I believe words would have been hurled at Hitler, Tojo and el Duce but nothing would have been done to stop their ways.

----

[2] I am speaking of the Jim Crow laws that will be discussed later.

Japan had defined the Pacific co-Prosperity Sphere with it ruling over and profiting from the area including Australia and New Zealand. Japan envisioned it as a twentieth century colonial empire not unlike the one created by Russia after World War II. Based on the treatment of Chinese and others during the war, it was no less oppressive than the Stalin's empire. Let's face it, that was what Hitler, Stalin, Mussolini, and the leaders of Japan individually saw, each having a colonial empire.

Although I would not have wanted to see it happen, suppose the US went out of the war and pulled back to the continent, Japan took the South Pacific and moved into Asia, Hitler took Russia out of the war and moved east, what would have happened when they met? All of this is possible, but I have never heard anyone from Academia consider it but then, it doesn't fit any of their narratives. Having studied the two regimes and the men who led them, the peace would only have lasted until one of them wanted a piece of the world the other held. Germany was working on an atomic bomb, admittedly well behind the US.   Japan did not have an atomic program, even at the end of the war. Had Hitler gotten the bomb and he was also working on long range aircraft. I have no doubt Japan would have eventually felt the heat of atomic fire at the hands of the Germans. Neither Hitler nor Tojo would have allowed anyone else to rule. Italy would eventually been like the Vichy in France. Admittedly this is conjecture but looking at the players, it is mor than plausible. I am not sure how long America would have stood on the sidelines had the Japanese not directly attacked American interests.

In contrast Hitler was both brutal in dealing with the German citizens, particularly those who were not "Aryan" and with those outside Germany. Even Aryans in Germany were at risk if they didn't get with the Hitler program. Hitler's concept was 'my way or the labor camps.' In all oppressive governments there are two underlying principals, staying in power and grabbing more power. It is really an addiction to power that drives most oppression.

The British Empire was nearly totally unlike others, but it generally had three levels of handling power and freedom. No matter where they lived, the "real British" were afforded many rights, the British subjects in the colonies were afforded some rights and those outside got whatever was dished out by whomever was in power.[3] Much is made of the caste systems in some countries but within the British Colonies there were 'caste systems' where those of color did not fare as well as whites. I hear statements that unlike America, the British did not have slaves. Check the treatment of non-white colonists. They may not have been slaves in name, but the term serf is not far from the truth. The locals had very little if any freedom. They had few rights and little protection from government abuse and even abuse from private citizens of British citizenship. This was particularly true for people of color. They were not hauled off as slaves, they were enslaved in place. One of the problems the British faced was American colonists who had been British subjects who now were being treated as second class. Once someone knows the sweet taste of freedom it is hard to get them accustomed to the bitter fruit of domination. The Crown learned that at Concord and later at Baltimore and New Orleans.

I will discuss this in detail because that empire worked in reverse to all others, it started out powerful and relinquished power but of course, not without some struggle and external incentive, i.e. revolts in the colonies. It was the Americans who began the process in 1776 and today the British Empire is one of the cornerstones of civil rights in the world. There are areas where a British Subject and an American citizen in their own lands will see greater or lesser freedom than the other but the overall level of freedom in the two are very nearly the same. I would not want to move to the Commonwealth, but the level of individual rights is not a part of that. I would at my age have to learn how to drive on the wrong side of the road. It is one of the things the British still have wrong. <grin>

I am sure some legal analyst will challenge my assessment of the relative freedom by mentioning something, possibly the difference in the death penalty but these impact very few and are pretty much the result of excesses of the individual citizen. Except for miscarriages of justice which are possible under any system, Americans and British citizens who have been imprisoned or executed by the courts committed horrendous acts. Although it took some years after the

---

[3] The account of the Apostle Paul shows this when he was taken prisoner in Acts 22:27. The Roman Soldiers were fearful of violating his rights because he was a Roman citizen. Before they knew that, anything goes.

Magna Carta, the threat of having one's head lopped off for offending the Crown diminished quickly. The other major colonial powers for the most part only relinquished power when it was ripped from their cold, dead hands either by other powers or revolution. The Spanish-American War served to dismantle much from the Spanish Colonial Empire including Cuba and the Philippines. Although the battle on San Juan hill is well known the crucial battle was the defeat of the Spanish Navy at the hands of American sailors at Manilla. It is interesting how a quest for power can cause someone to forget the past. Cuba became a sovereign nation on American shot, shell and blood. Sixty years later Americans were threatened with Russian nuclear missiles based on that island nation. Their falling under the rule of the Dictator Batista and then exchanging him for the brutal Castro were not the fault of the US except that we tolerated Batista without sanctioning him.

After the American Revolution Britain was slow to relinquish power, but it was happening. To their credit most of those former colonies are nations with respect for individual freedoms with exceptions being ones like Pakistan where there is a brutal Muslim influence that opposes freedom. We hear so much of the excesses in other Islamic nations, but Pakistan is far from a bastion of liberty. There is a Christian woman in Pakistan who is under a death sentence for her faith. Asia Bibi has been in jail since the 2010 sentence was pronounced.   The charge is not murder or terrorism or some other horrible crime, it is blasphemy against the prophet Mohammed. I have a question for the Muslims, what if Christians sentenced to death every Muslim who blasphemed the name of Jesus? I do not advocate this. I suggest it only in a hypothetical sense, to show the absolute lack common sense in the Muslim minds. Islam could easily qualify as a mental illness.

The British Empire

The British Empire was well formed by the time the Americans got riled up and dumped tea into the Boston harbor and fomented a revolution. There was a statement, "The sun never sets on the British Empire" meaning that the empire stretched around the world. With far-flung colonies and their support Britain was a formidable sea power. That was unsuccessfully challenged, first by the Spanish Armada and later by the German Navy in World War I and to some degree World War II with the large battleships and submarines, and the Japanese Naval air arm. The Repulse and Prince of Wales were sunk early in the war in Asian waters by Japanese planes while the American and British Navies still maintained that air power could not sink battleships. Until the encounter with the Japanese the British Navy had few losses, the most notable being the encounter with an American Admiral, not on the high seas but on Lake Erie during the war of 1812. Perry, with his three ships built of green wood, sailed by American sailors who the British knew were inferior, were up against a superior force and won. Although the British took significant losses in the World War I battles with the German Navy, they were the obvious winners. The Battle of the Atlantic against German submarines nearly forced Britain into surrender. Technical improvements including better sonar, microwave radar for aircraft, and convoying prevented that but only with significant sacrifice. Ironically, the implement of war, a British invention, the cavity magnetron that made the aircraft radar possible today exists in nearly every American home inside the microwave oven.

When the British tried to confiscate a cannon from the colonists, they were fired upon. Red Coats died along that road and within a few years the world had a new nation. Had that not happened I believe that something else would have triggered the war. There were too many firebrands who saw freedom from the Crown as the only option, they were vocal and respected, and the Crown seemed to not recognize that any repressive action only fueled the fire. They continued actions that only galvanized the colonists and made rebellion inevitable. Winston Churchill said that Americans can be counted upon to do the right thing after they have exhausted all of the alternatives.

America has never really been prepared for any war it entered except maybe the recent gulf wars and the revolution was no exception. We are like the football team doesn't start playing until they are 21 points behind. We won our independence, not because we kicked the British out but because they saw the war as a bad enterprise. I do not know if in the back of his mind King George had a plan. "Let them think they won. We will take them later." It is easy to prove that point. If you look at some of the British acts during the 1778 to 1812 period, particularly taking American sailors prisoner by committing official piracy on the high seas, an act of war, it looks like the British Crown had a long-term plan to take back the territory. As an aside, the war of 1812 ended with the treaty of Ghent which was signed in December 1814, before the Battle of New Orleans which was a devastating British land defeat at the hands of Colonel Jackson. It wasn't fought till January 1815. There was no instant messenger to tell the British and American Armies it was over, so Jackson lay in wait, the British attacked and as the song said,

> "we fired our guns and the British kept a coming.
> There wasn't quite as many as there was a while ago."[4]

I am not sure this is a hundred percent historically accurate but the reduction in British forces indicates it is not far from the truth. Jackson's men waited until they could "see the whites of their eyes" and then fired.

In the meantime, the British had burned Washington, bombarded Fort McHenry where Francis Scott Key wrote 'The Star Spangled Banner', killed a lot of Americans and as an aside, lost many of their own. Few have heard the verse of our National Anthem that excoriates the British. Yes, this is the third of four verses[5] of our national anthem. I have never heard it performed and in fact am not sure I have ever heard verses two and four either.

> And where is that band who so vauntingly swore
> That the havoc of war and the battle's confusion
> A home and a country should leave us no more!
> Their blood has washed out their foul footsteps' pollution
> No refuge could save the hireling and slave
> From the terror of flight, or the gloom of the grave,
> And the star-spangled banner in triumph doth wave
> O'er the land of the free and the home of the brave!

One of the lines there is of interest to me, the hireling most likely refers to the Hessian Soldiers who were hired to put down the Revolution. They were Germans who were mercenaries. One of my ancestors fought

---

[4] The song, "The Battle of New Orleans" by Jimmy Driftwood
https://en.wikipedia.org/wiki/The_Battle_of_New_Orleans
[5] The Star Spangled Banner https://genius.com/Francis-scott-key-star-spangled-banner-annotated

in the Revolution Army and another was a Hessian soldier who stayed after the revolution.

Although there was some activity on the Canadian border that could have been a major problem for the Americans had the Canadians, to be distinguished from the British residing in Canada, really entered the war. The Canadians really didn't have their heart in the war. They may have seen that their future good fortune lay in just letting things happen. Let the Americans take the British down a notch. Don't alienate your neighbor.

Like all neighbors Canada and the US have scrapped at times but over the years there has been far more good will across that border than any other international border in the world. I will admit that may be pragmatic. That is one very long border to fortify, something like 3000 miles, over 15,000,000 feet. Just putting two soldiers in one foxhole every twenty feet, certainly not an effective defense is a million and a half men. The French German border with the Siegfried and Maginot lines was only about 390 miles.[6] As an aside, the border with Mexico is 1954 miles or about 10,000,000 feet. The two men per 20 feet defense would take a million men to cover. We need the wall.

The British before the War of 1812 committed official piracy on the high seas. They would stop an American ship and take some of the men off and hold them. They claimed they were British Citizens. The treaty of Ghent specified that these be returned but some were not until five years after the war. Again, I mention, British Citizens had rights unless the government decided otherwise.

French Quebec

Canada, like most of the British Empire has a good record for human rights but the pseudo-country of Quebec has foisted its will and idiocy upon a whole country. Their pressure for the "bi-lingual" Canada has pressed on a large population the will of a small one. Canada, its provinces and its businesses spend millions on signs to appease the French-Canadian minority. They have laid a tyranny of the minority on the majority. Why should a business owner be forced by law to spend

---

[6] Source Wikipedia https://en.wikipedia.org/wiki/Siegfried_Line

extra money to put up a sign with the French translation if he does not want to? Maybe he doesn't want to deal with the French speaking people. Based on my experience I am not sure I would want to deal with them if I could avoid them.   And worse, under what perverted sense of fairness should he be fined if he does not? I see nothing wrong with it as a suggestion, not a law.

I will relate a true story that shows the idiocy behind the movement that instituted this travesty in Canada. Although it is one person, it shows the mind-set.

The day this bi-lingual oppression went into effect I was working in the computer field for Caterpillar in York, PA. I was working with a Canadian Cat Dealer to have them send their orders to us on computer readable media. Instead of them mailing us paper orders they had printed on their computer and us having to key the order into punched cards, they would have their ordering program punch the order into cards and they mailed them. Later they moved to writing a magnetic tape instead of the cards, reducing the mailing cost and even later this changed to connecting the two computers directly over a phone line but that wasn't viable at that time. The work we did on the first step made the later ones possible.

I needed to contact my counterpart there to discuss data formats and called the dealer. I could not dial his extension direct. I got a female voice that said, "Bonjour." I explained that I did not speak French and got an instant click of a hang-up. The law said that businesses in Quebec had to answer the phone in French. No problem. But it also allowed English to be used after that, probably the only common sense in the law. I called back several times with the same result. To say that smoke was coming out of my ears was not far from the truth. I was being pressed to make this happen and I now had an artificial roadblock. I found a phone number of the data transmission modem, the only other number I had and dialed that. I knew the chance of an answer there was small, but it was the only thing left before I resorted to US Mail and Canadian Post and the associated significant delay. I let the phone ring and ring, possibly 30 times and someone answered. It was not customary to answer a data phone unless you were expecting a transmission. Most calls were wrong numbers. This was before robo-calls.

The voice was tentative, "Bonjour." I thought, "Here we go again." I explained no French, she responded, "Little English, I get someone." It took some time, but another voice came on the phone, I explained the situation and the man told me he would have my contact call. That call came in a few minutes. I explained my experience and Bill told me he would call me back after he reported the front desk situation that needed immediate correction. I got a call from him about a half hour later. He told me to hang up and call back in. He asked that I call right away and if he did not hear from me in 10 minutes, he would call me. I called again, got again "Bonjour" and explained no French. The response was, "How can I help you." I later learned from Bill that he had reported this to his manager, who passed it to the president of the company. The president made a test call to the company number, asked for English and got the hang-up. Let's just say there probably was smoke coming out of his ears too, but he was in a position to correct the problem. I applaud him for doing the check, to know first-hand before acting. Bill explained to me that the woman who hung up on me was no longer in their employ. Let me explain the seriousness of this. What if I was a potential customer who wanted to buy a half million-dollar tractor, or maybe a fleet of them? I am sure the hang-up would not have positively influenced the customer to buy from this dealer. I also mentioned the woman who answered the data phone to Bill and asked that she be told she did it right and express my personal thanks. She seemed afraid she might be thought to have done something wrong when she answered the phone and I wanted to be sure she didn't worry. Although she apparently did not think she could help me she had me hold and got someone who could. He told me he had already advised her supervisor and his boss of her actions and both had complemented her on it, but he would pass on my thanks. I believe in both positive and negative reinforcement on behavior.

There is idiocy and there is common sense. All too often the idiocy is what prevails in making laws. Although there is some good in the Quebec French law, the overall is tyranny. The dual language signage in places where it enhances safety is more than a good idea, it must be done. I would see such a law here for Spanish on safety signs as valid but not a requirement for others. That it is government mandated except in safety situations is tyranny. Yes, I used that word. The law gave a person an opportunity to bring her political/social views into the workplace in a destructive way. It is fortunate that she, not someone else was the victim of her actions. I look at the National Anthem Kneeling at pro football games in much the same way. There should not be a law, but I can turn off the NFL if I like. Unfortunately, if that happens of too much, many who have jobs with the NFL and its peripheral, who are not a part of the idiocy will suffer too. With COVID this impact has been amplified.

The Confederacy

I am sure most who read this know the difference but there are many who do not differentiate between the Articles of Confederation which was the predecessor to our constitution, an imperfect document but a template for what could become a 'more perfect union'[7] and the Confederacy, the Confederate States of America, which as a rebel government was terribly oppressive and even more so was founded on oppression of a significant portion of its citizens. I do not wish to diminish the evil of slavery but to a significant degree the po whites[8] in the south were a portion of an oppressed. Although not slaves, they were oppressed by the leaders. I deal with this in detail in the book, 'The Balkanization of America'.[9] The po whites were fed the hate laced Kool Aide ladled out by the southern aristocracy and were moved to become cannon fodder to prosecute the war to continue slavery. This Kool Aid has been the basis of much of the division of the races that persists to today. We can debate from now to 2000 and froze to death whether the rebel states legally left the Union or whether it was over

---

[7] We the people of the United States, in order to form a more perfect union, establish justice and insure the blessings of liberty to ourselves and our posterity do ordain and establish this constitution of the United States. The preamble to the constitution giving the reason for the document.

[8] I hope I do not offend but the term was used in the era to denote the poor whites in the south. Less kindly terms like white trash were also used. The Southern Aristocracy had nothing but contempt for them, the same contempt they had for both the slaves and the middle class.

[9] 'The Balkanization of America', By Ralph Brandt available on Kindle.

Corn pone, Grits, States' Rights or Slavery but let us be very pragmatic. There was one and only one root cause of the action, the Southern Aristocracy wanted to preserve slavery. <u>If slavery had not been an ingrained social institution in the south, there would have been no reason for succession.</u> Without a reason for succession there would have been no war. Slavery was the one thing that drove every decision. <u>It was the root cause.</u> The blue blood of the southern aristocracy was as virulent as the Arian supremacy of Nazism. I would be remiss if I did not at this point mention that more Americans died in that war than died in all other wars the US has been involved in. If anyone thinks the American Soldier cannot fight, look to that. They killed each other with skill and ferocity.

Let us go one step further. Had the south let Fort Sumpter stand in Union hands it is likely that there would have been no war or at the least it would have been precipitated by some other action by the Confederacy. We may today have two nations![10] I we look at the directions with regard to liberty, those in the south, all but the blue bloods would have suffered. The aristocrats were in charge and they were no better than those who took the reins in Russia. You can argue whether the Union should have tried to hold or quietly given up Sumpter, but it was a Union military base and countries are reluctant to give up such an installation. Few counties have given up such an installation without a fight unless it could not be defended for some reason. Look at Bataan and Corregidor in World War II. A lot of Americans died defending them and more were marched off to Japanese prison camps. Many died on that march, called the Bataan Death March. Had the cannons not rung out there in April 1861 and heads had cooled for two or three years, or maybe even a few weeks, a treaty may have seeded the base to the Confederacy at some time for some other consideration, including one as innocuous as ending tensions, preventing conflict and starting diplomatic relations. Had the states of the Confederacy been content to succeed, form a nation, keep

---

[10] Maybe 3 or 4. Would the west have stayed with the union? Would Texas be a separate nation? Of course, that would have depended on finding someone willing to fight for their independence. Few of those killed at the Alamo were Texans. There were more from Pennsylvania than Texas and at least 3 other states had more than Pennsylvania.

its slavery, start negotiating seriously with the Union to normalize trade and diplomatic relations, and not started arming the border (as opposed to just establishing usual border checkpoints); I doubt war would have been the result.[11] Except for some anti-slavery firebrands, the Union did not have a dog in the fight and even when war broke out there might not be significant enthusiasm for it. In addition, the northern factory owners wanted southern agricultural products, particularly cotton and they were happy with the southern markets for manufactured products like those made of iron. The war broke off that trade and I am sure harmed business on both sides. The only good thing about the war for the northern industries was the need for the implements of war.

To give you an idea of this, a 6 gun battery of 3 inch Army Ordinance Rifles, otherwise known as ugly black cannons with a 3 inch bore that

were the staple of the Union forces, shown at the left, could in battle fire about 3 rounds a minute from each gun. In ten minutes, that is 30 rounds per gun, 180 for the battery, each shot was 9.5 pounds of iron and used about a pound of powder. A ten-minute barrage expended nearly a ton of iron and nearly 200 pounds of powder. The blast furnaces of Caledonia, Pine Grove[12] and others had to be busy to keep up producing the replacement rounds. So did the producers of charcoal, miners of ore and quarries producing limestone that fed those blast furnaces.[13]

---

[11] I have written two alternate histories based on World War II, 'The Second World War' that begins with a sea battle north of Pearl on 7 December 1945 and 'The D-Day Landing has Failed' where Allied armies were pushed off the Normandy Beach. I have never thought of one about others till I started this book. What if Sumpter was not fired on?

[12] There were high grade ore deposits all over Cumberland, Adams, Franklin, and York counties and there were iron works near many of them. I mention only a few here. One at Caledonia was owned by Thaddeus Stevens. It was burned by the Confederate forces who went from Gettysburg to Chambersburg to burn and loot.

[13] These are the things that go into a furnace to produce iron.

The powder factories were also busy as were wagon makers, weavers, and others making the implements of war. Although the north was cut off from the southern agriculture the North's agriculture was sufficient to feed the population and the army. Just the manufacture of these guns was significant. Over 1,100 of them, weighing 820 pounds each and with a carriage that weighed 900 pounds required well over 1 million pounds of iron.

The south had little if any industry and most important, iron production, so a significant amount of their supplies had to come across the Anaconda, the union blockade or be bought secretly in the north and smuggled across the Mason Dixon line. Maryland, a border state had many southern sympathizers. The border was not the Mason Dixon Line, the southern border of Pennsylvania as many think. That line had much earlier resulted from the British settlement of a border dispute between the descendants of Lord Baltimore and Willian Penn. As an aside, Mason and Dixon the low bidders to the crown to set the border when the case was settled. They were <u>astronomers</u>. They set the border using star sights. They were not surveyors as we were told in school. They did a very accurate job, few of their markers are far from the line when verified by the best GPS. At least a couple of the ones that are not close have the appearance of being moved.

When Sherman marched to the sea, he had his men tear up a stretch of every railroad they crossed, usually about a quarter of a mile. He understood the south's economic situation. Sherman's orders to his men was to not just tear up the rails, a team of gandy dancers[14] would repair it in a short time. They destroyed the rails and ties, so they could not be used to rebuild the section. The smaller pieces, the nails, bolts and fish plates were parsed out to the troops to be carried and dropped into streams and lakes as they traveled. Although these contained small amounts of iron, it was necessarily high grade and they were labor intensive to produce. The railroad ties were pulled up and used to build fires to heat the center of the rails red hot, then they were picked up by two groups of soldiers and bent around the nearest trees before the troops moved on. These iron pieces were called Sherman 'bow ties'.

---

[14] Gandy dancers is the term for the guys on the track laying crew who drove the spikes. Two men worked together driving a spike. It was almost a dance.

These could only be removed by cutting the tree or the rails and the rails were not useable except as scrap to melt down. The southern ironworks did not produce any rail during the war. These rails were almost impossible to replace with the blockade and ties cost labor that the Confederacy was short on due to men being away in the war. Many look at the march to the sea as brutality to the south. Sherman's tactic was to cut the south in half with respect to transportation. With that done supplying an army was becoming more difficult. While the Union was expanding and improving its railroads under a unified plan, the Confederacy was being deprived of its. Realistically the South started a war without the ability to prosecute it unless they could win quickly. Such is often the short-sighted view oppressors take. We often hear Lee lauded as a great general. I liken him to Admiral Yamamoto who at Pearl said, "I fear we have awakened a fearsome giant and given him a terrible resolve." He knew Japan must win quickly or lose. Whether Lee saw that or not, I don't know.   But it was just as true. Yamamoto knew they had about six months to totally defeat his enemy or he would rebound. In both cases they were not able to win quickly and the wars continued, both for nearly four years. In both cases the aggressor weakened as time went on.

Sumpter brought the issue to a head. Later Confederate advances made peace impossible. Once blood was shed there was no way back.

Let it be clearly shown, the south was a viable society, but the life-style of the aristocracy of the Confederacy existed only because of slavery and to continue it. You can talk states' rights but the only right of a state that was in question was the preservation of slavery. Had cooler heads prevailed in Richmond it may be the Capitol of a nation to this day. The decision to fire on Sumpter signed the death warrants for many Americans and the Confederacy as a nation. Whether the states had the right to succeed from the union is debatable. That they could not make it happen was the issue that was settled on the battlefield.

And because of that for four years the cannon rang out across the land. Bullets took down many of the young men. It may be well to note that the number of Americans killed in that rebellion, let us recognize it, was so great that if we were to total the number of men killed in all other wars America fought the total would be less. The oppression of the Confederacy ranged well beyond its borders, both in territory and time.

Although the Confederacy died in 1865, it had roots that did not. They were just repressed. Vestiges of the Confederacy exist to today. Tyranny and oppression are hardy concepts. They are difficult to root out. They were held at bay during the reconstruction but with the advent of the progressives like Teddy Roosevelt and Woodrow Wilson they rebounded in their desire to court the southern Democrats who were for the most part, the descendants of the aristocracy that caused the war to preserve slavery and were no more enlightened than their forefathers. Many had hatred for blacks, they saw them as the cause of the war and their parents' removal from power. We will discuss some of these later.

Lincolns Government

Lincoln is often held up as the paragon of virtue, he was a great man, but his government had some black spots. The Union during the War of Southern Rebellion got somewhat oppressive as do all countries under stress. Many revere and almost worship Lincoln. I respect and honor him for the good but question some things. I remember men often do things that are driven by their time and society and I deal more-kindly because of that than some others do.

Conscription was used to raise an army. The necessity is hard to refute. Let's face it, the armies of the Confederacy were knocking at and in some cases crossing the southern border. It looked like an emergency. But after Gettysburg the war went far beyond defense. Many of the battlefields were in Confederate territory. It is hard to claim a battle fought in Georgia or Tennessee was to defend the Union from Confederate aggression any more than the excursions into Maryland and Pennsylvania by the south were necessary to prevent "northern aggression" which was the term the southern leadership used to whip up the po whites. That war was called the War of Northern Aggression by the firebrands in the south. <u>The early battles would correctly be called by anyone who was objective, Southern Aggression.</u> It was part of the propaganda campaign to prosecute the war. During and for about twenty years after the war, the north called it The Recent War of the

Rebellion, an accurate term but the political correctness police changed it to The Civil War – the term I learned in school. It was an attempt to make the south feel good and hides the real issues.

Admittedly the battle of Gettysburg was defensive and Meade's lack of pursuit of the Army of Northern Virginia after the battle, a pursuit that might have allowed him to devastate a broken army before it had an opportunity to reform and recover, showed how defensive a stance Meade took. To paraphrase Churchill, Gettysburg was not the end, it was not the beginning of the end of the Confederacy, but it was the end of the beginning. Lots of blood remained to be spilled in the next two years.

Even Lincoln, a politician not a military man, saw the fallacy of not pursuing the enemy. Lincoln knew it had to be done or the war would continue. Lee's Army had to be soundly defeated, not by repelling an attack but by devastating it. In Meade's defense, he had seen the carnage of the battle first-hand and knew the state of his own army. He did not know the precarious state of Lee's forces but the bodies on the battlefield and in particular the litter from the devastation of Longstreet's Charge, incorrectly called by historians 'Picket's charge'[15] should have indicated that. He did not need an accountant to tally the bodies. He had only to look across that field and see the number of bodies and wounded in grey to know the Rebel Army was badly mauled. Just the bodies along fences at the Emmitsburg road would have been enough to note that. Sure, his army had seen significant losses, but it was relatively intact with units intact enough to be able to trail Lee and fight. More units could have been committed as they were given a day or two to recover. Sure, the units on the ends of the union line, Culps Hill and Little Round top, and the ones in the middle, at the apex of Picket's Charge were badly mauled. But many other units were relatively intact. But they and the Union artillery had taken a terrible

---

[15] Picket commanded only about one fifth of the men who crossed that field. It is called Picket's charge because of a Virginia Newspaper article. Picket had a friendly reporter who recorded his view of the battle and noted how Picket's brave Virginians crossed the field. He ignored the other four fifths of the attacking force. The whole force was under the command of Longstreet and it would be more accurately called Longstreet's Charge.

toll on the Confederates. Lee lost about 25,000 of his 75,000 men in the three days. The union losses were about 23,000 of about 104,000. While Lee had about 50,000 men, Meade had over 81,000, however in the fog of battle, that superiority may not have been apparent.

I firmly believe it was more the overall view of the death and destruction on the battlefield that emotionally prevented him from the pursuit. Meade's heart failed him. At that point in time he just couldn't bring himself to order more men into the caldron of combat. If you doubt this can be a factor in the mind of a military officer, look at the second day of the Battle of Gettysburg. Lee has created a rolling attack, (as compared to the one massive assault on the third day) seven units, about three regiments each, about 3000 men in a group, to cross the valley in front of what is now the Pennsylvania Memorial.[16] It would start with the first attack on the Confederate right, if it ran its course and failed to break the Union line the second would move and if it failed the third would move in and so on.   The Union was able to repel the first six assaults but at that time the Union front at the seventh attack point was very thin and there were no more reinforcements to throw in. Every reserve had been used to stop the previous attacks. Many were killed or wounded, many were short on ammunition[17] and none were in any position to support the defenders if the seventh attack came. So critical was the situation that the officer on the hill had already used the Pennsylvania Third Artillery like infantry to stop the one attack and the under-strength Twentieth Minnesota with about 160 effectives[18] (compared to about 1000 of a full-strength regiment) was thrown in to stop 3000 screaming rebels on another. When the next reinforcements were sent in behind the 20th they were told to not expect anyone but Rebels in front of them. The 20th had been written off. The advancing Union troops found there were still over a score of the Twentieth, some wounded, still holding the line! The defensive line broke but the 20th

---

[16] I knew little of the second day until I spent some time at the PA memorial and a fantastic Battle Historian, Eric Campbell walked up and started telling about the battle. This man has been a resource and on camera for several History Channel programs.
[17] The standard issue of ammunition for a Union soldier was only 60-80 rounds.
[18] A full-strength regiment was nearly 1000 men. The 20th was one sixth of a regiment facing three full regiments of screaming rebels.

had been able to stem the flow and prevent a Confederate breakthrough till reinforcements arrived.

This operation that up till now failed to open a hole in the Union line would have almost certainly succeeded had the Confederate commander on the seventh attack ordered his men forward. His attacking force would have greatly outnumbered the defenders who would get no support. At least one artillery support unit, the Pennsylvania 3rd was still reforming from the effort to stop the third attack and too far away to help. The confederate officer had seen the carnage to his right, men being hit by Minnie balls, shot and grape.[19] He could not find the strength to order his men into that valley of death. His courage failed. For the lack of that order the Union line held, the battle went on another day and had he ordered them forward and his whole force of about 3000 been wiped out which was unlikely, had the Union line failed there, and it almost certainly would have, Longstreet's Charge with much greater losses to the Rebels would never have happened. The Union line would have been split near the point where the Pennsylvania Memorial stands with Confederate units rolling it up. A Union withdraw, most likely rout was inevitable at that point. The Confederacy may today be singing, "We chased the Yankees all the way to Harrisburg." Meade missed the same kind of opportunity on a much larger scale. Had he pursued Lee the war that began in April 1861 may have ended in two and a half years, late 1863 rather than in four years in April of 1865. Had Meade lost most of his army in the pursuit it would have been far less than the losses in the later campaigns. Had he killed every retreating Confederate soldier in the process the losses to the Confederacy would have been less than they were in the war. The Patton doctrine of warfare was validated here, you expend men and shot now to avoid expending it later.

---

[19] Grape, also called canister is a thin walled can containing iron balls, each about the size of a large grape. It is fired from a cannon to stop an attack when the enemy is near, about 30 yards out. It is like a giant shotgun. The pressure of the powder explosion rips the can open and spread. With the number of projectiles, it generally cuts a hole in the advancing line.

But for the lack of an order the war was simply to drag on. And the oppression grew. There were draft riots, more conscription and more suffering.

Although the South complains of Sherman's March to the Sea as noted in the song, 'The Night They Drove Ole Dixie Down'[20] one must remember the country was at war and they say war is hell.[21] In an episode of the TV show Mash, Allan Alda's character Hawkeye says, "They say war is hell. They are wrong. War is war and hell is hell and war is worse." Although theologically I know hell is worse, in one sense the statement is true because hell is meant for those who transgress, war catches up a lot of innocents. In fact, many of the perpetrators of the war too often go Scott Free. Many of the perpetrators of The War of the Rebellion were allowed to have their heads go down to the grave in peace.[22] In no other country would this have been allowed, the perpetrators of the rebellion would have faced a firing squad, a noose or even worse. When I muse over this I am reminded that there is a Holy God, a Righteous God and He is the final judge who knows the hearts of men.[23] That final judgment is decided in a court where a slick

---

[20] The Night They Drove Ole Dixie Down - Written by Robbie Robertson.
[21] In the mind of General William Tecumseh Sherman, who made famous the phrase "War is hell," there was no doubt as to the integrity of the North's cause. Wikipedia.
[22] In King David's instructions to his son Solomon when he was about to die he said.
1Ki 2:5 And also you know what Joab the son of Zeruiah did to me, what he did to the two commanders of the armies of Israel, to Abner the son of Ner, and to Amasa the son of Jether, that he murdered them, and shed the blood of war in peace, and put the blood of war upon his girdle on his loins, and in his shoes on his feet.
1Ki 2:6 And you shall do according to your wisdom and shall not let his gray head go down to the grave in peace.
[23] Mat 25:41 Then He also shall say to those on the left hand, Depart from Me, you cursed, into everlasting fire prepared for the Devil and his angels.
Mat 25:42 For I was hungry, and you gave Me no food; I was thirsty, and you gave Me no drink;
Mat 25:43 I was a stranger and you did not take Me in; I was naked, and you did not clothe Me; I was sick, and in prison, and you did not visit me.
Mat 25:44 Then they will also answer Him, saying, Lord, when did we see You hungry, or thirsty, or a stranger, or naked, or sick, or in prison, and did not

lawyer cannot get you off on a lie or a technicality. The guilt is measured by actions that are accurately noted.

As bad as the oppression perpetrated by the Confederacy was, the legacy of it was far reaching and may have been worse.

Czarist Russia

When the powerful heap to themselves opulent and lavish lifestyles the result is certainly the oppression of others to pay for it, even if it is no more than high taxes. It is frequently true of Royalty in many cases as well as commoners who gain power by ability. Somehow power-drunk people forget the lot of those they once were, the ones who helped them depose the previous tyrant. Monarchies have varied in human rights from the British Crown that was very good after the Magna Charta placed limits on it to ones like Czarist Russia. There was some sympathy for the children of the Czars that were brutally treated during the first Russian Revolution and I for one do not see they should have been. I also look at the comparable group, the children of the southern aristocracy who continue to this day to heap injustice on others. Maybe the Russians had it right. But then, they settled for a more brutal taskmaster, Communism.

I also note that the stage was set for this by the treatment the population got at the hands of the royalty. When you sow to the wind you often reap the whirlwind.[24] The Czars dealt badly with the people and when the people got the opportunity they retaliated. This is one of the things that happens during a revolution. People drunk on new freedom want to cleanse the landscape. They also know that the old leaders may have a following that could organize and rally around the deposed leader and take back the reins of power. Even the children of

---

minister to You?
Mat 25:45 Then He shall answer them, saying, Truly I say to you, Inasmuch as you did not do it to one of the least of these, you did not do it to Me.
Mat 25:46 And these shall go away into everlasting punishment, but the righteous into everlasting life.
[24] Hos_8:7 For they have sown the wind, and they shall reap the whirlwind: it hath no stalk: the bud shall yield no meal: if so be it yield, the strangers shall swallow it up.

the royal family could be that spark. Few of us have ever been in that kind of position and it is hard for us to play out the thoughts and emotions that surround it. I have had a picture into it by seeing a report on the Hungarian Revolt against the USSR in Budapest in 1956. They for a short time threw off the Communist yoke only to have Russian Tanks and troops smother the revolt. The report was an interview with one of the men in the revolt who was killed a short time later by those USSR forces.

With the Czars deposed there was somewhat a void of leadership and order and a struggle for whom would ultimately take power ensued. In that chaos came another struggle. It was the White Russians, the non-communists against Red Russians, the communists.

Communist Russia

Let us begin by setting one item of the record straight. Communist Russia is not and never was a <u>Communist </u>nation. If Marx saw what came about in the name of Communism in Russia, Cuba, China, etc., he would be adamant. This was not what he envisioned. His vision as laid down in the Communist Manifesto was a society that had resources that were contributed by everyone based on ability and were disbursed to everyone based on need. The strong party organization was only to exist until they taught the masses how to live in unity and the party was the vehicle to show them how that would happen. Martin Luther King Jr. had a dream. Karl Marx had and documented a nightmare. It was a great vision with one very serious flaw. Marx was not the great thinker and philosopher he is touted to be. He was a political hack who had an idea and never looked at the consequences. He had a myopia that he alone could create a model for a perfect society. The 'Marx Plan' ignored history and there is a wise saying that those who ignore history are condemned to repeat its mistakes.[25] Actually, it should talk about those who work to not make the mistakes of history because many repeat the mistakes even when they know. The Apostle James wrote in James 4:17, "Therefore to him who knows to do good, and does not do

---

[25] "Those who do not learn history are doomed to repeat it." The quote is most likely due to George Santayana, and in its original form it read, 'Those who cannot remember the past are condemned to repeat it.' Wikipedia

it, to him it is sin." Too often we know what went wrong, we just repeat it. The Apostle Paul in his letter to the church at Thessalonica wrote:

> 2Th 3:10 for even when we were with you, this we did command you, that if any one is not willing to work, neither let him eat,
> 2Th 3:11 for we hear of certain walking among you disorderly, nothing working, but over working,
> 2Th 3:12 and such we command and exhort through our Lord Jesus Christ, that with quietness working, their own bread they may eat;
> 2Th 3:13 and ye, brethren, may ye not be weary doing well,
> 2Th 3:14 and if any one do not obey our word through the letter, this one note ye, and have no company with him, that he may be ashamed,
> 2Th 3:15 and as an enemy count him not, but admonish ye him as a brother;

Remember when reading this passage that Paul was a follower of teachings of Jesus, you are your brother's keeper, and at other places admonished to do good to all men, to love unequivocally, and care for the widows and orphans. But sometimes there must be balance and he was addressing a problem in a church were people have decided to not work and sponge off the others. Even in this very closed and caring environment of the early church, things went wrong. Looking at the failure in that environment there is no way it would work on a wider scale. Marx's utopia was a pipe dream that has become a nightmare for many.

We then go to one of the early American settlements, Jamestown. Captain John Smith issued an order that those who did not work did not eat after the colony nearly starved because many were not working. With Smith's mid-course correction of the plan, within two years the colony was eating well and prospering. Again, Marx's theory did not work in even a closed environment. It is hard to believe Marx did not have knowledge of these, but if he did, he ignored them. Like many of the socialists of today, he had an ego that enabled him to say, "I am smarter than they are. I can make it work where they failed." The

COVID situation has created massive handouts in the form of unemployment. There is now, a few months into it, a concern that the payout is attractive enough that some are not seeking to work. The idea is good, provide for people. The result has issues. There are other examples, too many to include.

Marx, frustrated by what he saw around him and to some degree his own situation and looked at only one side of the equation, the idea that this benevolent system he envisioned would be great. It would be if it was workable! He failed to look at the impact of human greed and laziness and more important how people who would grab power would see his ideas as a medium to enslave others. If you promise a utopia you can get followers. We are seeing this in the socialist movement in the 2020 election. Free anything sells to the masses who do not realize a Ponzi scheme only works for a time.

His writing has created what is probably the largest slave population in history, people living under communist dictatorships. Even with the fall of the Soviet Union the number has not decreased significantly because of where the cancer was spread. China, Cuba, Venezuela and others are examples. If the leadership of these was not living in luxury while others live in slavery, I could give it some good marks. It is interesting today that leftists in America will look at the socialist and communist societies as being better than the one in America and point to the deposed institution of slavery while ignoring the far greater slave populations that exist today! Where are the abolitionists who desire to free these slaves? Let me be blunt. They are not in the ranks of the left wing of the US government. For an example I point to Ronald Regan. Remember, "Mr. Gorachev, tear down that wall." Ultimately, he freed more slaves than Lincoln.   But then, both were Republicans. Note that socialism is a stepping-stone or better slippery slope to dictatorship, just look at Italy and Germany after World War I. We will deal with them later. That slope is greased by corrupt politicians, self-seeking media, celebrities with no understanding of things outside their gated communities and the masses who have been dumbed down by the corruption of the American Education – or better mis-education system by leftists who have painted socialism as good. They have perfumed and put a shirt on a hog.

With the promise of getting rid of the abuses of Czarist Russia and installing a benevolent society the Communist Party in Russia was able to create a cadre that produced a revolution that first removed the Czars and then placed the Communists in power after a second very bloody civil war between the communists and non-communists in a fight that included some American and British forces that were in Russia at the time supporting the White Russians, those opposed to the Communists. Once the Communists won it took no time for these who talked so benevolently to become hostile and oppressive. I am sure there were some among the communist ranks who helped because they honestly saw this as producing a better society, and let's face it, the Czars were not the most freedom friendly, but I am also as sure that there some in the communist party who saw this would become a place of power, authority and even wealth for them. I have studied various movements in politics and religion and have seen that in 'revolutions' it is all too often that the power grabbers are the ones who grab the power and control after the previous regime is deposed. The ones who saw it to better people generally are not the ones who grab the reins and they are pushed out. In cases where a dictatorship comes to power they are usually killed or sent to prison. They are idealists who may become a threat when the evil of the dictatorship becomes apparent.

I will give two instances from the United States, a counter-example and one that supports the thesis. It is possible for things to go right but history tells us the odds are against it. Most revolutions replace one oppressive government with another, usually more oppressive than the first. The American revolution is an exception.

The leaders of the American Revolution quickly put in place a pre-Constitution, the Articles of Confederation that put limits on government power and then about a decade later replaced it with a constitution that set those limits more explicitly. The refusal to approve the constitution without the Bill of Rights, the first ten amendments is solid proof of that. These provided rights to the citizen including the fundamental freedoms and limits on government. Imagine the US without the constitutional guarantees of freedom of the press, peaceable assembly, redress, religion, and speech? What about the protection from self-incrimination, (5), unreasonable search and seizure, and the right to bear arms? Although I have never heard a teacher mention this it is very clear to me that the founding fathers feared someone with less pure motives would come to power and there needed to be checks and balances, but it may be possible that they feared that even some of their number could be tempted.

On the other side of the coin, we have a fantastic example in the 1960's Civil Rights Movement. When Martin Luther King Jr.[26] was killed there was a void at the top. This is always a good time for someone greedy for power to grab the reins. There was a man who was a student of King, a man with vision like King and who had spent time with King who was also possessed the humility King carried. I look at him like Elisha who it was said of that he poured water over the hands of the prophet Elijah. He and Elisha served the man they followed. You may never have heard his name, Ralph Abernathy[27] because the press concentrated on the firebrands who spouted vile and evil rhetoric and with the press exposure they rose to the top. The press went the sensational, i.e. what sold papers and air-time. I firmly believe both blacks and whites in America would be better off if Abernathy had been the heir to King. As far as I know he has been in some role in Civil Rights since and there has not been a hint of a scandal associated with him. He just isn't flashy enough to make sensational news reports. Unfortunately, absence of scandal cannot be said of Jessie Jackson,[28] Al Sharpton,[29] John Lewis[30] and Louis Farrakhan.[31] None of these have served the civil rights cause well. We must remember, scandals sell. As P. T. Barnum said, "There is no such thing as bad publicity." The media continues to report on those who grab power.

---

[26] I find it incumbent on me to give that date April 4, 1968, Memphis, Tennessee. His net worth at time of death, $250,000 – about $2 million today, not a great sum.

[27] Ralph Abernathy Net Worth is $850,000 – at death in 1990. Comparable to Martin Luther King Jr.

[28] Net worth – $10,000,000

[29] Net worth - $500,000

[30] Net Worth - $300,000 Remember John was getting a US Senator salary and perks.

[31] Net Worth - $3,000,000

In Communist Russia, by design of the leadership or by necessity of the weakness of the flawed system it quickly migrated to a dictatorship. No dictatorship is benevolent. If we read Marx, all of him, not just the nice parts, the communist party will have to exercise control as they teach the masses to live in unity. That is a nice way of saying there will be a dictatorship. It must oppress to maintain its grasp on the society and the people. Once it grabs the reins it holds them tightly. There is no timetable, no sunset clause to their power. (It is why I believe all laws on the books except maybe murder and treason should have a sunset clause.) They will keep it until they see fit to release it. Once drunk with power, it will not be released.

The Russian Communist Party grabbed the reins hard and held them, not only oppressing their own citizens but also those of surrounding countries and some far flung like Cuba. I have not studied a dictatorship that has not quickly become oppressive enough to imprison and kill its citizens for 'crimes against the state', the euphemism for violating the laws of the dictatorship or asking embarrassing questions and often many are killed because of their position or even that with their education they may become a problem for the state. They can even be killed on a whim. There is no presumption of innocence. I also cannot find one that has not threatened their neighbors. Oppressors oppress.

Hitler had many leaders of the SA, the organization of nearly a million that had been the security force for Nazi events killed in the 'night of the long knives'. There seems to be no reason historians can find except that Hitler felt the SA <u>could</u> become a problem and he might have to share power with the SA leader. Some historians believe Hitler was fed false information about the SA by people near him to gain his favor but that has weak evidence. With the 'night of the long knives' the SA was effectively disbanded with many of the members being integrated into the SS and military.[32] Hitler had eliminated a possible challenge.

In like fashion in the thirties Stalin had many army officers sent to concentration camps with just as little evidence, an action that proved

---

[32] The actual number of deaths is not great, but they were carefully targeted to remove the effectiveness of the SA.

to be short sighted when the war with Germany began and there was a shortage of trained and competent middle grade officers. Roughly 20 million Russians including these officers were sent to concentration camps and less than half of them survived.

Look at the action of another Communist enclave. When they took over the south the Vietcong killed many teachers, government officials, and educated persons <u>and their families</u> because they may become a problem. There the concern was they would be ones who could lead an opposition. The oppressors see no value in letting any possible opposition force exist.

One common thread here is the concern about these being a nucleus for an opposition or a revolt. This has two background items. Governments with intense control, i.e. dictatorships, want to stamp out any opposition quickly and even prevent it from forming. Killing potential dissidents does that and serves to remind others that this behavior will be met with extreme force. Remember, most of these governments came to power by revolution. They see the possibility and do not want to allow someone to go down that road. The exceptions here are Hitler and Mussolini who pretty much used the democratic process to gain power but circumvented it at times with the use of violence and threats where the process did not seem to be working their way. Another thing that oppressive governments hold dear is that the end justifies the means. All too often the means is removing opposition by any method including death.

It is well to note here that after one death occurs for expediency the next death, the next ten, the next hundred, the next thousand and even the next million is just numbers. Even loyal members of the society are at risk if it is expedient to have them disappear and this includes even those in the inner circle if others in it see them as a risk. Some of those who were killed in Vietnam were sympathetic to the Communists, but the death orders were by class, not name. Dictators tend to not be careful with expending resources, including disposing of people if it promotes the cause. North Korean dictator Kim, a.k.a. Little Rocket Man has had even family members killed to consolidate power.

It is apparent from history that Communism only works where there is strong government control, i.e. a dictatorship. Something that always comes with strong government control is oppression and end of personal freedom. Although it may take some time it eventually becomes pervasive. Rarely is that word eventually measured in units more than weeks, even when not, months.

In Communist Russia to maintain the lavish lifestyles of the leaders of the revolution, resources were diverted to the elite to the extent that the some of the farmers in the countryside, the people who were growing the food, were starving. The farmers did not have enough to feed their families. Couple that with the central control by bureaucrats who knew little of farming that dictated bad planting times which resulted in crop failures and the country was soon in a government-created disaster. Dictators routinely think they know best and push their ideas on the people. Hitler's forces may have been able to repel the Normandy Invasion on June 6, 1944[33] had his tank commanders on the scene had been free to make tactical decisions. Hitler was so sure that the invasion at Normandy was a ruse that he held his tanks to the north to oppose the 'real invasion.' I did an in-depth study of this when I wrote a novel, 'The D-day Landing Has Failed'. There were two Panzer divisions that could have driven between the British and Canadian beaches and gotten to the beach, cutting off the armies on those beaches from their supplies. One of the fears I have today is the propensity for the left in the US to be so sure they know best. Is this a pre-cursor to dictatorship?

But with the government control of the media and communications information the causes of the famine and hardship never got to the masses. With the level of control and the suppression of any form of dissent and no ability to impact policy the idiocy continued for several years. Even talking about government problems could bring the forces of the government down on a person. Talk of winding up in Siberia was not an urban legend or a joke. It happened to anyone who could be considered an enemy of the state. Any negative talk could be defined as such. A comment could buy you a ticket to Siberia.

---

[33] See the alternate history novel, "The D-Day Landing Has failed" By Ralph Brandt.

Even by 1972 Russia was not able to grow enough wheat and corn to feed its population and turned to the US to buy grain.[34]

Russia's Grain Up 15 Per Cent

MOSCOW (UPI) — Russia's grain yield this harvest is running about 15 per cent behind last year's poor crop because of the century's hottest and driest summer in the Ukranian breadbasket, official statistics revealed yesterday.

The disclosure by the Central Statistical Office threw light on an unexpected meeting of the Soviet leadership nine days ago to discuss the harvest and the purchase of additional grain abroad.

Western diplomats reported Russian buyers were scouring the world's grain markets for wheat and other fodder grains available for delivery this year.

The government newspaper Izvestia reported that with most winter wheat harvested, the Central Statistical Office estimated average yield in the Ukraine this year was 31.4 bushels per acre.

It is interesting to note that in more recent years with less government interference as the government released control and moved to a more capitalistic economy, the Russian farms are producing enough grain that they have become a grain exporter, raising concerns on European farms that these exports would hurt their business and prices. With the relaxing there is a note here that Communism not only doesn't make things better, rolling it back does. The government that resulted does not grant the level of personal freedom we have but hopefully it will improve, not regress. It is unfortunate that a significant level of corruption exists, mostly fueled by the communist influence. This is destructive to the average Russian.

Communism values people like you would a cheap hammer. It is to be used, when it is no longer serviceable, it is discarded. During World War II many daughters of party officials were enlisted as military pilots.[35] In the thirties many party member daughters were trained to fly, just as elites in Britain and the US learned horseback riding. With pilots in short supply they were given minimum training in warfare including fighters and bombers. They were given the worst planes and sent out. Many did not survive.

One of these and her wing person attacked a German formation of 5 fighters. By now they were flying planes that were more closely

---

[34] Tampa Tribune August 18, 1972 – not the headline states "up 15 percent" while the article correctly states, 15 percent decrease.

[35] The White Rose of Stalingrad: The Real-Life Adventure of Lidiya Vladimirovna Litvyak, the Highest Scoring Female Air Ace of All Time Author Bill Yenne Publisher: Osprey Publishing; 1st edition (February 19, 2013)

matched with the Germans. They shot down two of the Germans but in the fight the one plane was damaged and the pilot retreated from the fight. Her leader covered her retreat but was unable to disengage. The wing person returned to base, the leader did not. Because she was not seen being shot down, here plane was not found and she did not return, <u>she was listed as a deserter and her family was not given a settlement.</u> Around 2000 a hiker in a rugged area found a plane, it was the leader's plane and her remains were there. Fifty-six years after the battle she was removed from the list of deserters.

Socialism

Socialism is not necessarily oppressive, it is less so than communism, but it is too often the slippery slope that is started upon and once the slide starts it ends only in oppression. There are examples of nations in various states of this slide. One of the great philosophers said, "The road to hell is paved with good intentions." The road to oppression is often paved with cobblestones of socialism placed there by either the well-meaning or the power-hungry. Both are the enemies of freedom because they create a society that has an almost narcotic dependence on the system. When you are dependent, you are a slave to the provider, i.e. the government. It is what I call 'feeding the bears.' When you are in public forests you are told, "don't feed the bears." There are two reasons. If you feed them and then quit, they may become hostile. In addition, too much feeding may make them forget how to forage for food. The same seems to happen under socialism. Some, in fact too many, become dependent on the government and quit working. When an attempt is made to stop the dole, they get hostile. This has happened in many socialist and communist countries.

The apostle Paul mentioned that in a letter cited earlier. In addition, the government becomes oppressive to those who are working, demanding more and more taxes and further killing incentive, making it more likely some of those may quit working and become dependent or learn more effective ways to avoid taxes, causing the system to spiral. Eventually the government must become more and more oppressive to keep enough people working. The system oppresses both the beneficiaries of the system and the benefactors. Many of those benefactors would engage in true charity but resent the government mandate to 'help the poor and needy' too many of which are not really the poor and needy, but are ones who are lazy, greedy and are working the system.

Socialism may start out good but always moves oppressive and it is a one-way street.

Even those who would implement socialism can be oppressive when they are working to create their fantasy of Socialist utopia. We are seeing this now in the US in its neo-socialism.

Social Security has created a population in the US that does not plan for its future thus not providing a reasonable support system for the future. Too many think; "the government will take care of us with Social Security." The maximum Social Security benefit today which is not sustainable, the system will run out of money some day – is about $2,900 dollars a month. Medicare takes $135 of that and a decent Medicare supplement and drug plan takes over $300 – and that with a $500 deductible amount. The #34,800 per year is reduced by more than $5,720 in just medical coverage. This leaves less than $2,500 a month – and most Social Security payments are in the $1,500 a month range, weaving $1,000 for living. In 1968 Medicare was added and under GWB we added prescription drugs. I am surprised that Bernie Sanders or Chuck Schumer have not suggested government supplied pet care and auto insurance.

But they have advocated free college tuition. I would agree to that if the socialist college professors agreed to work for free. Allow me to show a real-life situation that shows what government intrusion does. In 1965 I graduated from Shippensburg State College, now Shippensburg University of PA. It sounds more impressive, a mandatory academia principle based on socialist leanings. Names must be impressive. We can't have it called 'The Cumberland Valley State Normal School at Shippensburg', the name it has when founded. It got the more impressive names, 'Shippensburg State Teachers College', 'Shippensburg State College', and today, 'Shippensburg University of Pennsylvania.' None of these changes in name made one iota of difference in the quality of the education except maybe the one that took it from 2 years to four, and I will submit that the education quality today is less than it was in 1961 when it was SSC. I understand the partying is better. My tuition for the last full year was $300 with an activity fee of $45. I just looked up the 2017-2018 fee schedule. My activity fee today including Student Union would be $757 – up 16.9 times – far more than the roughly 9 times for inflation. The tuition is over $5100, again up 17 times. By inflation the cost should be 9 times 300 or $2700! But the government got involved, more regulations, more subsidies, more requirements and student loans that made the field of students larger, the money pool larger and the gains more. Instead of operating a frugal business the state colleges went lavish with facilities, unconscionable professor salaries driven by unions, staffing with non-productive personnel for all kinds of idiocy, and the like. The US has moved from the land of the free to the land of the freeloader. They are not all on welfare as we know it, many are on government subsidized positions that look good but are essentially welfare. And they exist wherever Socialism gains because as government grows, socialism hides excesses.

But Socialistic portions of government need not run this way if the proper management is in place. In 2000 I was working with a telecom contractor on a project for the Commonwealth of Pennsylvania. I was in a meeting with the Secretary Richard Browdie, the head of the PA Agency on Aging – certainly a 'socialist oriented agency'. We were working on the options of his agency's phone upgrade. In the three-quarter hour meeting there were a couple questions he repeatedly asked. "Will this provide better service to the people we serve?" "Will this make it easier for my people to do their jobs?" "Is there a lower cost way to accomplish this?" At one point he commented, "Every dollar we spend on this is a dollar I don't have to help the people." If every head of every government agency had those four sentences in his mind, even if they didn't hit 100% on carrying them out, government would serve us better and cost less. I will tell you that although I am not sure the agency served the Commonwealth the best, the right process existed to get it. If those concepts are in place, most of the time it will be the best, on occasion it will be nearly so. I do not expect perfect government. I just want it to work to be better. Socialism always moves away from that.

I will digress her to show government idiocy. Keystone Building was constructed in late 2000. About one third of the space is a mezzanine, a useless space. Had that been utilized, several agencies that were in other buildings that were awful, most of them rented, could have been relocated there. I can think of an agency on South third and several on the 100 block of Pine Street that were in what I would have called, dumps. Were they not government buildings they would have failed L&I inspections for safety. Two had restrooms on half floors, to get to them you had to do a half flight of steps or go to the ground floor. There were fire safety issues in all three! I was in each for a few days, was glad to get out.

I would be remiss if I did not mention something else about Secretary Browdie to show the caliber of that man. About half -way through that meeting his shared secretary (the top three men shared 2 secretaries) popped in and whispered something to him. He quickly excused himself and left. He came back about 10 minutes later and explained. One of his people (about 160 in that office) got a call that one of her children was in an auto accident and was being taken to the hospital. He considered his leaving the meeting briefly to offer support to her and be sure she was being taken care of was his duty. He apologized to us for leaving but considered it essential he do that. I left that meeting wondering why this man was in charge of an agency with 160 people, why hadn't he been entrusted to lead one with 6,000 or more. Government's job is to care for people, the populace and the workers, all of them. Secretary Browdie understood the mission better than any other cabinet member I met.

But socialism and communism do not attract this kind of people. They attract those who wish to climb the ladder.

Fascist Italy

Many see Mussolini as an underling or offshoot of Hitler. He was not. He took over Italy in the early 1920's, more than ten years before Hitler came to power in Germany. He was well established in Italy when Hitler was still lurking in the back streets of Germany. Hitler looked at him as a role model. Only on the battlefield did Hitler not see him with respect. Like Hitler, Mussolini was not right wing, _he was a socialist_. After consolidating power by legal means, he destroyed free speech and became a dictator. He not only oppressed his own people, he reached out to neighbors and beyond. At one point he called the Mediterranean an Italian lake and claimed for Italy islands that were never part of Italy.[36] His incursion into Ethiopia seemed to show an impotence of the Italian Army but with German support Italy was able to hold territory in North Africa for some time.

EXPANSION THE POLICY OF THE NEW ITALIAN PREMIER

Mussolini Regards the Mediterranean as an Italian Lake and Advocates Complete Control of That Waterway by Italy —Has Always Bitterly Contested the Claims of Greece for the Dodecanese Islands—New Ministry is Hostile to Extreme Socialists and Communists—Fascisti Troops Have Triumphantly Entered Rome.

Least I convey an error, the Italian Army's impotency on the battlefield cannot be laid at the feet of the average Italian soldier. They performed as well as any when provided with adequate training, equipment and leadership. The British learned this when confronted with pockets of Italian forces that were under the proper leadership, even when they had less than optimum equipment. The Brits were in for a tough time when they hit one of these units that decided enough was enough.

In a like manner the Germans tended to view American soldiers the same way, mainly at the result of Nazi Propaganda. At some point the Nazi leaders started believing their own propaganda, a dangerous thing. The German propogandists said Americans were soft, would not fight. They somehow ignored the American civil war and the American presence in France in World War I. Things were going very badly in World War 1 for the British and French when the Americans arrived. Sure, the numbers were important, but the American soldier was a formidable foe on the battlefield. There are many stories of heroism like the one of 'The Lost Battalion' that was the only unit that was advancing in an attack. It got ahead of the flanking units on both sides and was surrounded by Germans. Their losses were significant but the German bodies when they were relieved showed that the Germans paid an awful price and were unable to dislodge them.

The average Italian soldier, given proper support was formidable. But the oppressive government gave them mostly bad leadership, mostly by

---

putting political hacks in officer positions. One of the worst oppressions is sending a man into battle without giving him the best chance of survival possible. Allowing politics not capability as a criterion for appointments to leadership is oppression.

Nazi Germany under Hitler

It was Adolf Hitler who said, "Tell a big enough lie, often enough, and everyone will believe it." Lies have been the staple of oppressive governments. When it isn't going well, they find a scape goat. For those who do not know, the term 'scape goat' goes back to Jewish Ritual. Two goats were selected to atone for the sins of the people.[37] The priest would kill one goat as a blood sacrifice and the other, the scape goat, he would lay hands on to impart the sins of the people to it then release it to the desert. It was to carry the sins of the people away from them. Hitler found his scape goat, the Jews. An article shown later will prove he had that idea that Jews were the problem from as far back as 1920. As he rose to power, he blamed all of Germany's ills, financial, business, the World War I loss, on the Jews and told the German people that the way to German supremacy required that International Jewry was to be eliminated. As he consolidated power this allowed him to bring about the programs that would "settle the Jewish question." That program resulted in the deaths of over 6 million Jews. Least there be any doubt, the holocaust happened. But will add, many others Hitler saw as inferior, the Slavs, Poles, etc. suffered just as severely under Nazi rule.

In a recent discussion with a friend she asked a question. "Did Hitler really believe the Jews were responsible for the ills of Germany?" Although I find no information that clearly shows his intent I responded with "yes". By the time Jews were being slaughtered Hitler had consolidated power. It would have been easy to not run the extermination program, which incidentally cost Germany resources to carry out. The resources to build and operate the camps and gas chambers, the soldiers to man them, these could have gone into the war effort. The loss of the human resources as Jews were killed certainly did not help the war effort. Sure, some of them were put in

---

[37] Leviticus 16:21-22

slave labor camps but I doubt that had the positive impact had these being at home and working. Hitler had to believe the Jews were the enemy to carry out the extermination program. We see these myopias in quite a few situations in the war, his mindset that the invasion of France would be at Calais, the opening of the Russian Front, and others. When Hitler got an idea, it was to be carried out. Few questioned him, those who did were subject to extreme prejudice.

I encountered an article in The Gazette (Cedar Rapids, Iowa) · 31 Mar 1933, Fri · Page 4. It is an article 'Gruenwald Recalls Visit with Hitler.'

Grunewald, who saw stirring times during the fascist revolt in Italy, predicts that Hitler will strike a snag by attempting to play Mussolini in Germany. He believes that Germans are not the kind to be long ruled by a dictator. Persecution of Jews will likely be a boomerang, Grunewald believes. The Germans have become accustomed to free speech, a free press and freedom of action; they will soon chafe under the yoke, in his opinion.

That visit with Hitler was in 1920 when Hitler was a <u>sign painter,</u> not an art painter as I was taught. The full article is Appendix 1 if you wish to read it. I will note that this man who met with and discussed things with Hitler for over 2 hours felt thirteen years later that the Germans would never allow Hitler to become a dictator! History proved him wrong. Reading this I have even more concern about America. Could we 'want the trains to run on time', the problems of our country, to be so blind as to sell our freedoms? I will answer that for you, you can see the answer in November 2020. If the socialists win the presidential election and both houses of congress, we are headed to a dictatorship.

It is interesting to note and is covered in detail in the book, "The Alt-left the New McCarthyism" that Nazism is not, repeat not, right wing. It is the radical left on steroids. The lie of right-wing designation for Hitler and Mussolini was concocted by the radical left as an attempt to show that Hitler was not a Socialist. They felt these two made socialism look bad. Allow me to crush that. Nazi is the short name for a party that was the 'National Socialist" party. How a party with the name 'Socialist' can be called right wing is another lie of those who would oppress us with a socialist society. The Hitler government had many socialist programs.

Hitler's government oppressed its neighbors starting with lands that were annexed before the war started, some annexed by the treaty Neville Chamberlin carried back to Britain and proclaimed, "Here we have it, peace in our time." War was just a few years in the future and would continue for nearly 7 years.

But before the neighbors were oppressed, the German people became his first victims. They would also be his last. It was said in Germany in the mid-1930's that under Hitler, the trains ran on time. The German people traded freedom, admittedly not a full one, for the man who promised he would cure all of Germany's ills. As I look at it, the cure was worse than the disease. It ended with Germany occupied by its enemies, divided, and devastated. Hitler said to the German people, "Give me power and I will fix your problems." For a time, it appeared he would do that. The German people were his last victims, the Allied armies and air forces were the instruments to carry it out.

Although I know he was not the anti-Christ, he had some of the characteristics. It is interesting that in early 2018 I am looking back at 2008 and remembering similar promises by another socialist, Barak Hussein Obama. Many fell for the line and voted for him. We are now seeing exposed civil rights violations that are horrendous. But to socialists, the end justifies the means. The goal is a society they control.

The super race and International Jewrey were slogans to bring him to power.

Imperial Japan

Imperial Japan must fall high on the list of oppressive governments, both at home with its own people and in its colonies. Most of these colonies would not be listed as such by historians because they will be listed as lands conquered during World War II like the Philippines and parts of China but there were lands that were subjected before that war. Japan has a long history spotted with brutality to its neighbors. In the 1590's Japanese forces wished to march through Korea to attack China. The Korean leader refused and the Japanese occupied Korea in three months. There has been bad blood between Japan, China and Korea for at least four centuries. Japan has for the most part been the aggressor. The culture of oppressing neighbors and a national elitism and ethnic superiority is well ingrained in the Japanese psyche. It goes back to at least the 1500's. In some areas, mostly commercial, the elitism exists to this day in spite of the defeat in World War II. American leftists who lash out against America for its concepts of manifest destiny are strangely silent when there are other countries, particularly those with a socialist bent, take such an approach. Even Japan's actions in bringing the world to war in the Pacific are buried under the cries against America for the use of the Atomic Bomb. That bomb would not have been created in a crash program without the war. The two bombs that were dropped on Hiroshima (August 6, 1945) and Nagasaki (August 9, 1945) resulted in 240,000 deaths. The Japanese slaughtered millions of Chinese. The devastation came home to roost. Japan, the aggressor had fewer civilian deaths than its neighbors. To liberals it is okay for Japan to brutally murder 25 million Chinese civilians (and about 5 million of other nations in the area) but not for the US to kill 240,000 Japanese to end the nation's murdering its neighbors. They strain on a gnat and swallow a camel.

The Korean Admiral Yi was able to win battles against the Japanese Navy[38] in the 1590's and cut off the Army supply lines to China. When Japanese leader Hydeyoshi died in 1598 the army withdrew from Korea and Japan temporarily took on an isolationist stance.

During World War II Korea fought with Japan but there are questions about how much of this was forced by Japanese occupation. I see this almost as I do the Finns participating with the Axis in the European theatre. They had little or no choice. Few know Finland was an Axis nation. Much animosity still exists between Japan and Korea to the extent that there is hostility created by Korean references in Japanese history books. In addition, there are charges that Korean women served as 'comfort women' for Japanese troops and it is not clear if these did so willingly or were enslaved. It is likely that latter is the case and this view is held by most foreign historians who tend to be more objective than the locals. It would not be surprising since this was done in other occupied countries.

---

[38] There is a great movie 'The Admiral' that shows the defeat of the Japanese armada in one of those battles.

Japan continued its conquest of the area during World War II including significant parts of China and then expanded to the south Pacific as far as New Guinea. The American landing at Guadalcanal, sea battles off Savo Island and the Battle of the Coral Sea were instrumental in stopping this southern expansion. Even after devastating defeats as we moved up the islands the Japanese did not surrender. As we ended Japanese occupation of the various islands and defeat loomed the Japanese people suffered under the war conditions. They saw sons go to war and not return.

The Japanese occupation and its treatment of both civilians in the captured areas and captured combatants ranged between oppressive and brutal.   The Bataan Death March that occurred early in 1942 showed the brutality that Japanese Military would exert on captured soldiers. The treatment of the survivors of Wake indicate some surrendered only to be executed. The story of captured airmen as mentioned in Gregory (Pappy) Boyington's book, 'Baa Baa Black Sheep'[39] details cruel treatment gone to seed. The German treatment of captured airmen was far from cordial and could easily be called harsh and even some of it inhumane, but generally and except for the worst abuses it paled when compared to the treatment of POW's by the Japanese. Boyington was for some time in a hut that held seven other men. All seven that were there when he was placed there died and some of the replacements died before he was taken out and sent to Japan. The best accounts say that about 33% of American soldiers that were captured by Japanese survived and were repatriated.[40] Based on personal accounts I have read I would have suspected it was not nearly that high and may be tainted by the Japanese not reporting some POW's for weeks and months, and if they died, reporting them as killed in action, not POW. I will mention that many Germans who were taken prisoner were housed in the US in over 200 camps, some in South Central PA. One camp was at Michaux, near Pine Grove Furnace. It had several satellites and together they housed over 2000 POW's. Of those, all but one survived the war. He died of hanging, either at his own hand

---

[39] There are other accounts of the brutality. The accounts of the men captured at Wake align with the ones by Boyington.
[40] Wikipedia

or by fellow prisoners, what my dad who worked with him believed. Sgt. Georg Hartig, mechanic, father, RIP. I am sure there were German prisoners who died after capture, either from wounds, illness, or in escape attempts, but the number was small. Records show that 96% were repatriated. Many of them worked in farms, fields and factories, were paid for that and returned to Germany with at least some money to start a life.

With the lack of medical care for wounded POW's it is likely many were alive but died before being reported. I will temper this lack of food and medical care with the comment that the average Japanese soldier was enduring much deprivation in the same combat areas however there was no justification of the brutality that contributed to the number of deaths. It seems that the Japanese soldier had an idea that if American POW's were beaten it somehow made the Japanese stronger. In comparison accounts of American civilians in the Philippines show harsh treatment with many not surviving the nearly four years of occupation. The local civilians in the area were generally allowed to go on about their business but any resistance or lack of support of the war, real or perceived was met with harsh treatment, often death. Many of the deaths were carried out on the spot without even any formality or pretense of juris prudence.

Enforced labor on the China-Thailand railroad resulted in the deaths of 12,600 Allied POW's and over 120,000 local laborers.[41] Although the US had some POW's working in fields, factories and forests, they were volunteers, well fed, worked reasonable hours, paid for the work, and many wanted to stay when the war ended. At least two in the Cumberland County Michaux prison camp escaped in January 1946, a month before they would have been repatriated to Germany, hoping to be able to hide and stay.

Most historians list the local laborer death statistics in the Far East much higher and I tend to believe them. Most of these were forcibly taken from their homes and simply worked till they dropped from starvation and disease. Those who could not go on were often

---

[41] Wikipedia The Death Railway Most historians believe this figure should be close to two million.

summarily killed. The Japanese did not consider these 'inferiors' worth counting.

In China Nanking was hard hit by Japanese brutality and the estimate of the number of dead varies from 50,000 to 300,000! That variation in the number varies shows the Japanese attitude to the Chinese and other peoples they considered inferior – which was anyone not Japanese. While Germany kept accurate records of the killing of Jews, the Japanese did not bother counting deaths of non-Japanese. Many of these were driven into the river because in the Japanese mind a 'Chinaman' wasn't worth a bullet!

But Japan's lack of concern for human life extended to its own. The Pearl attack took the lives of nine of ten midget submarine crewmen who thought they were on a suicide mission. The survivor was in a sub that ran aground and was captured before he could commit hari-kari. Kamikaze pilots flew off as human bombs. Banzai charges threw hundreds into the US Marine machine gun fire. The tactic was an old one, if enough men were thrown at a single point in a defensive line, some of them would survive and breach it. The body count was not a concern. Japanese Aircraft had few safety items, for example American fighters had an armor plate behind the pilot to protect him and self-sealing gas tanks to reduce the chance of fire. That saved many American pilots including Robert Johnson, one of the highest scoring aces who early in his career landed in England with a shot up P-47 that never flew again, but he did. There were seven 20 mm cannon shells and several dozen machine gun bullets in the seat armor. Had even one of these hit him it was unlikely he would have survived. Even a wound from one of the smaller bullets could have been fatal with the long flight back home. One of the 20 mm cannon shells would have almost certainly been instantly fatal. Think about a bullet more than ¾ of an inch in diameter going through a body. There are dozens of stories like this. The US also spent much more in Search and Rescue of downed crews. In the economics of warfare, saving trained and experienced men is prudent. It is weighed against the cost of replacement and most important, the experience of these men is almost irreplaceable.

One of the exceptions in the American arsenal is the M-4 Sherman tank that was basically both a big target and a death trap. The high profile made for being spotted. The armor and gun were both deficient and it used a gasoline engine which meant it carried gasoline. With the gasoline, one hit and it caught fire. It was called the Ronsen, named after the cigarette lighter that had the slogan, 'lights up first time, every time.' As bad as the gun and armor deficiencies were its ability to out-maneuver the German tanks and the ability traverse the gun fast and get off early shots would have mitigated the weaker armor if it had a decent main gun. It did not. There were alternatives for the gun, the Brits bought many of the M-4's with no gun and put on their 6 pounder that ripped German armor. They were called fireflies. The M-4's 75 mm 'armor piercing' shells more often than not bounced off the Panzers. The way to kill a Panzer was to get behind it where its armor was thinner but think about what the German gunner was doing while you did that. We had a shaped charge shell that could have been adapted to the 75 that would have consistently gone through the Panzer's armor, but it was never implemented. This shell in a much smaller versions, 37 and 57 mm pierced almost any armor of the day. An upscaled version would have been even more effective. Even a sabot round with the 37 mm would have been fantastic. Many of the encounters of a Sherman with a Panzer started with the Sherman getting off the first and sometimes even the second shot before the Panzer could get off one because of the Panzer's lack of maneuverability and slow traverse rate but too often it ended with a burning Sherman because the two shots bounced off the Panzer armor. With a better gun, the advantage would have tilted heavily to the Sherman. If you get can off the first shot, get a hit and the round is effective, it is unlikely the enemy will fire even one shot.

Early in the war, before the Kamikaze which appeared, Japanese pilots with damaged planes often crashed their planes into Allied ships. It was based in Japanese tradition, not policy of the government. In addition, the Japanese planes were relatively delicate and did not continue to fly with battle damage. The US had that problem with the P-51 that had a liquid cooled Merlin engine. (British engineering!) A pilot could have one bullet got through the radiator or a coolant line, the coolant would be lost, the engine would overheat and would stop in a short time. Most of other US planes used air cooled R series radial engines that were far more robust. Some of them continued to run and brought the pilot home with several cylinders shot away. The attrition of Japanese pilots eventually reduced the cadre of experienced pilots and that became a significant factor in the war. This practice only served to drive that attrition up. While many American pilots survived because planes with even moderate and sometimes severe battle damage made it home to fight again, most Japanese pilots in damaged planes died, either because the plane failed, caught fire or they crashed into an allied ship on purpose. The man who returns from the fight has the lessons learned to both use in the future and to pass on to others. Even late in the war when the Japanese and German industry was under heavy assault from the air, generally there were more planes than pilots and while the American forces were producing more new pilots and more of them were experienced survivors of previous battles. Most of the experienced Japanese pilots were gone by the time of the Marianas Turkey Shoot and many of the few remaining ones were killed there.

On the civilian side the Japanese Government had the people believing that the Americans would do despicable things so much that on one island thousands of Japanese civilians jumped off the cliff at the end of the island to prevent being 'captured' by the Americans. The rhetoric against surrender was so bitter that several Japanese soldiers did not surrender until the 1960's. They hid in the jungles under terribly primitive conditions for about twenty years, waiting for the Japanese Navy to 'recapture' the island.

We hear significant questioning on the use of the atomic bombs on Hiroshima and Nagasaki. These were raids I wish had not been necessary but when we judge it is well to look at the situation as much as possible from the eyes of those who were there at the time. We should consider what were they facing not what is nice to propose in a safer environment. I will discuss the likely outcome.

On one side America had been at war for three years, 7 months and 29 days when Colonel Tibbits and his crew, flying the Enola Gay dropped the bomb on Hiroshima, somewhere near 400,000 American soldiers have died, many more were wounded, and the country and rest of the world are tired of war. I can see a president being impeached for not using the weapon. On the other hand, regular raids were being made on Japan by B-29's carrying mostly incendiaries, fire bombs that were burning Japanese cities to the ground. Fire storms were killing Japanese civilians. Several of these raids each killed over 100,000 civilians. In some, relays of B-29's kept the fires burning for days.   Remember that number when you judge the use of the atomic bomb that killed about 120,000 in each of the raids. When you talk of tens of thousands of deaths, the exact amount is just numbers. You are killing people. On the morning of August 6, 1945 there was no Japanese diplomatic discussion aimed at ending the war. The overtures to the Russians came after August 12. Even Hiroshima did not trigger the action. They were still committed to fight till victory. No quick or even near-term end to the war was in sight.

The civilian population was being conditioned and trained to repel an Allied invasion that was expected and in fact that invasion was planned and preparations were under way. Japanese civilians would join the military and oppose the landing. I can assure you; this defense would have been a disaster for Japanese civilians.

A significant portion of the Allied landing forces were experienced troops, men who had been blooded and hardened in places like Guadalcanal, Tara, Iwo Jima, the Philippines, to mention a few. They had seen the result of atrocities by the Japanese forces against captured Americans and the civilians. Fervor ran hot for Japanese blood, and any Japanese blood would do. If we had put these men ashore under battle conditions, have them opposed by both the Japanese military and civilians , Japanese blood would have been spilled, lots of it. Any resistance from civilians would have been dealt with quickly and harshly. I have looked at the Allied casualty estimates for the invasion and have come to one conclusion, had the invasion been launched, Japanese blood would have been spilled freely. If civilians had joined the defense they would have been killed at any indication of resistance or threat to the Americans. Couple that with the continued fire-bombing of Japan, the 240,000 deaths at Hiroshima and Nagasaki may have been cheap for the Japanese. These attacks ended the war in less than two weeks without the invasion. They ended the war and ended the fire-bombing. It gave the Japanese military a way to surrender and still save face. Hiroshima and Nagasaki were sacrificial lambs, sacrificed by the Japanese leaders' desire to save face. I might note that Germany could have saved a lot of German civilian lives had they quit four months earlier. With Russia rolling up German forces in the east, American and British bombers in the skies, and the Americans and British now rolling into Germany in the west, it was time to throw in the towel, but Hitler sacrificed more Germans. It is ironic that Hitler committed suicide while the Emperor of Japan who nodded yes to go to China and Pearl survived the war, retained his status in the palace and his son succeeded him! He left the throne in 2017 and his son, the grandson of Hirohito is on the throne. Say thank you Douglas McCarther who would not try the Emperor for war crimes.

I will mention a couple other points here. Many put the atomic death toll much higher. They count nearly every person who died in the next 50 years who had been at one of these cities. I examine these kinds of statements. First, some of the people may have died early due to harm to their bodies by radiation, fire or physical injury. But there is no indication that taking out the ones killed directly by the bomb and those who died in the next month of injuries the life spans were significantly reduced. There was a small increase in the incidence of some cancers which would be expected. This number is regrettable but is far from the numbers thrown around.

In all of this we must remember, Japan went to war with the world. The bible talks of sowing to the wind. The result is a reaping the whirlwind. Japan went to war with the world. It set out to oppress other nations and in 1942 was in fact carrying that out. Much of the south Pacific and some of Asia were in their hands and they were administering those areas brutally. They sowed war on their neighbors. The war came home. It is regrettable but at times our actions bring consequences.

South Africa

In 1948 a white government took control of South Africa and initiated apartheid. Blacks, a majority, were relegated to near serfdom. I will not spend time discussing this in detail except to say it was Twentieth Century Dixie on steroids. Movement to racial equality came only with outside pressure, primarily sanctions. It is interesting how the fortunes change. White farmers in South Africa now live in fear because of black

actions. Sure, the blacks were oppressed but do two wrongs make a
right?

Others

I would go into the many other governments that oppressed including
The Vichy French government which only served as a puppet for Nazi
Germany as did the puppet governments in Norway and other captured
lands. Many of the North Africa governments' oppression stemmed
from the influences of Islam and the colonial powers. I covered this well
with other countries. In most cases the citizens were no better off after
they threw off the colonial fetters. In the places with strong Judeo-
Christian influence has oppression been placed somewhat in check.
Where Islam was able to take the lead, the oppression deepened.

One thing we must remember, freedom need only be lost once. Can
you imagine the cost of throwing off a government today with the
weapons available to them? You only need look at the devastation in
Syria today (2018) where an oppressive government is being challenged.
Look at the devastation in Iraq where ISIS was being displaced. We
must never allow this to happen here.

Saudi Arabia

One of the most bi-polar regimes in the world is Saudi Arabia. Most
other Muslim countries subscribe to similar idiocy, but they seem to be
the most adept at it. Males, one half of the population, enjoy some
reasonable form of freedom while women, the other half, live under
some of the strictest controls anywhere in the world. I find it ludicrous
that the left-leaning main-stream American and European press is
lauding the country for the relaxing of rules on women when they are
less than half-way measures. But then, they treat Communist Cuba the
same way. It appears that the left can excuse oppression if it is carried
out by Communists or Muslims.

In 2017 it was announced that women would be allowed to drive cars,
but not till June of 2018.[42] Why not now? Will they be more competent
drivers then? I could understand if it required the same testing to drive

---

[42] The Baltimore Sun (Baltimore, Maryland) 27 Sep 2017, Wed Page A1

Move is one of reforms prompted by young Saudi prince

BY NABIH BULOS AND LAURA KING
Washington Bureau

BEIRUT — Saudi Arabia announced Tuesday that it would begin allowing women to drive next year, a groundbreaking lifting of a ban widely seen as emblematic of the conservative kingdom's repressive treatment of women.

State television and the official Saudi Press Agency said the change to the longstanding practice had been mandated by royal decree and would take effect in June 2018.

Saudi women are subject to some of the world's strictest gender-based social codes, forbidden to exercise many basic rights without the permission of a male guardian.

But women for years have been seeking to defy the ban, which is enforced by denying female Saudis any means of applying for a driver's license. Some have been jailed or otherwise punished for daring to get behind the wheel.

The official Saudi news outlets said a panel would be formed to look into how to See DRIVING, page 15

that men must pass. The law is also changing that they will be allowed to go to sporting events but may only sit in the 'women's and children's sections.' They tout these advances but fail to mention that these same women are still prevented from having many other freedoms. Many of these rules are to 'protect' women. I have two questions, from what and whom? The basis of these rules comes from historic male domination that was based on women being weaker, needing protection, not being as astute, not able to survive without a man and needing male guidance. These same news people who cry for the rights of gays and transgenders being able to use the bathroom of their choice, a nicety by comparison to this kind of oppression and for a miniscule portion of the population, can ignore rampant discrimination against half of a nation's population. It is likely that there are more women in Saudi Arabia than gays and transgenders in the world[43] and there are other Muslim regions that have similar anti-women discrimination! Much of this discrimination has its roots in the archaic and hateful political system created by Mohammed and masquerading as a legitimate religion. The real nature of this hateful system is only hidden to those who are willfully blinded by their closed-minded ideas. I am not sure if it is insanity; a hatred for God, hatred for America or anything Judeo-Christian; or the left-wing agenda that approaches insanity that closes their minds to the truth. These tend to, I might add they seem to be suicidal. I find it incongruous that the radical left will demonstrate against neo-Nazis while supporting Muslim governments

---

[43] Not true, the world population is 7.7 billion, the population of Saudia Arabia is 28 million, 14 million females. One percent, of 7.7 billion is 77 million, roughly the number of gays and transgenders.

that have the same focus, wipe out Jews. Those neo-Nazis may have killed a few Jews, regrettable for sure, but the Muslim governments are in league with terrorists who have killed thousands, possibly tens of thousands of Jews in the last century while the Muslims point back centuries at the injustices against them, some real and many imagined. I also shake my head when I see American Jews flock to the polls and vote for left wing Democrat candidates who lend this support. If the Mores are able to subjugate America and install Sharia law here, those Jews, those in the entertainment business and politicians will be among the first to be killed.

If these restrictive rules are to protect women the question is germane, protect them from what? If there is a need to protect someone, there must be some threat. There are only two things it could be, the women's own actions are self-destructive or the men around them must be the threat. I could understand if they were allowed to do anything in their own country where the males are mostly Muslim and are according to Muslim folklore, restrained, pure, and holy. I say that with tongue in cheek since I know better.   Let the folklore continue. It is apparent that only when they come to sinful places like Boston to hijack airplanes and kill infidels that they get drunk and have lap dances with the women of the infidel. Only when they go to other countries claiming to be refugees do they rape. They do not do that at home. Really? Are Muslim men that easily corrupted to ignore the faith? Is the weakness of the Muslim man, his inability to control his passions really the reason for the idiotic clothing Muslim women are forced to wear and the rules they must follow? When Mohammed and his followers instituted this there were few non-Muslim men in the area. I believe in modesty, not insanity. I could really understand the concern if the woman was coming to New York, Washington DC or Hollywood where predators in the entertainment, business and political systems lurk to violate women. There they need a strong man to protect them. Based on the recent news I believe it would be prudent for any woman to wear a chastity belt in those areas of the United States, locked on with no way to remove it, full time. These three cities in particular, two of them heavily liberal and the other leaning precariously to the left, seem to be hostile to women. They cry diversity, gender equality but behind closed doors it is not so. The evil is done in secret. Worse it looks like this has been going on for twenty, maybe even sixty years and there has been a code of silence and a history of payoffs to hide it. I wonder how many of the actresses, including ones who are claiming they were assaulted, have gotten to the top, paying for their fame with their bodies and their silence. They are at least accessories and probably conspirators to the oppression. By allowing their violation to go unreported and unpunished for all these years they opened the door for more to become victims. Now they are screaming. Is it buyer's remorse? Is it a way to grab a sixty second spot on TV? Go figure. Sometimes the victims are also the victimizers.

And let's look at the idea of segregating the women and children from the men at sporting events. Is it really to protect them? You must have at least a couple screws loose to believe that. Where would they be better protected than sitting next to their big, brave Muslim husband with his AK-47 along with his three other wives?[44] He would be there to protect them if a right-wing terrorist from America wearing a shirt with a Confederate flag, his MAGA hat takes in his AR-15 into the stadium and tries to shoot up the women's and children's sections. Wouldn't it be best to have the men in that section to protect them and overpower him? With the factions in Islam, I do not rule out the women and children being at risk, but it will be someone from another Muslim sect, not a good ole boy red neck American Terrorist. I might bring this to the front by saying, the current spate of bombings in Afghanistan are not carried out by American Red Necks nor are the attacks in Iraq. They are carried out by Muslims, attacking Muslims. It is 'friendly fire.'

Some of the sects would oppose women in the events and might carry out such an attack. In the warped Muslim mind, any action they disagree with can be resolved using violence. The number of deaths doesn't matter if Allah is pleased. It is like the ancients that sacrificed their children to the gods. I know for sure one thing. If such an event happens, I am almost certain it will not be a good ole boy from Alabama waving a Confederate flag. They have better sense and better things to do. It seems that young Muslim males have nothing better to do than

---

[44] I had not thought of this until Anne Zarlinga, a friend, noted it. I thought it was good insight to include. I find wisdom in many places.

kill people. It is what they are brainwashed to do. It is a sad
commentary on their religion.

Allow me to insert a dose of reality. The Muslim men aren't concerned
about an attack by a red neck American because there has never been
an American terrorist involved in killing in Saudi Arabia, particularly
American southern boys who enjoy hunting game in the woods and
shooting beer bottles and targets, not people. There is something
exciting about seeing a bottle go into a thousand pieces in a way it
never will unless hit by a 30.06 bullet. Even a .22 will do something
worth watching.

They can't say that about a Muslim terrorist shooting up a place in the
US. Sure, those southern boys do stupid things at times like every group
of people, but they don't strap on bombs and kill people. For the most
part the stupid things they do generally risk their lives not the lives of
others. They may act a little crazy at times, but they are not afflicted
with the mental disease called Islam that says it is not only fine to kill
the infidel, it is demanded by Allah. Anything goes if it is for the
furtherance of the faith. For those who do not know, the infidel
extends beyond Christians, Jews, Hindus, and Atheists, it can extend to
Muslims that don't exactly follow the same form of Islam. It has a lot of
kinship with Nazi Germany's idea of eradicating Jews and other inferior
races. After all, every infidel is part of an inferior race and Jews are
particularly inferior. We must remember, the Jews and Christians are
the ones who rejected Mohammed's teachings and turned him bitter
and hostile to them because they would not convert. In Christianity,
that admittedly has been perverted at times and been less than loving,
we are to show love to that one who is not of the faith to bring them
into the Kingdom of God. Islam teaches to do it by lies and if necessary,
if they do not respond to the teaching, violence. Yes, there is a verse in
the Koran that says lying to the infidel in the furtherance of the faith is a
virtue. It is not only permitted, it is encouraged. The suicide bomb and
AK-47 have replaced the sword as tools of Islamic evangelism.

On the other hand, we have terrorists from Saudi Arabia or have been
trained there who have killed Americans by crashing planes, driving
trucks into a crowd, or shooting up a place. At one time we had to bow
and genuflect to these because we were dependent on their oil. Piss

them off and they close the tap. It is time for us to tell them we no longer need them. We are still supporting with American aid countries that are producing terrorists who want to kill us. This must stop. It is time to turn off the tap that spills American money. Like the bears when you stop feeding them, there will be repercussions.

But we avoid offending them because American companies have investments there. As bad as that reason is, we have a left-wing, anti-business group that is in league with them. They see Islam as a 'culture' and to promote 'diversity' and it is honored as a valid world culture and religion by this addle headed group of Americans, in fact it is worshipped. If you see Islam as evil, you are Islamophobic. I think these liberals should convert to Islam, go to Saudi Arabia and live. I will chuckle when I think of female performers having to wear the Muslim dress, not partake of alcohol and need a male relative to accompany them.

Unlike the liberal loonies I see evil clearly. It is not Islamophobia, it is a pragmatic, hard -headed, realistic view. They seem to enjoy killing. They want to kill me. They need to be stopped. If they wish to come and join our society as responsible members, they are welcome. They can even keep their worship of their false God, but they must be willing to live in peace with others. Oppression of their members and others must stop. Sharia and oppression of women must end.

Allow me to show a perspective. I believe the various groups in the world have brought good things to the American culture. The Chinese, Japanese, (and I mention them first for a reason, they rank high in those who were exploited) Italians, Irish, French, Germans, and others including the Africans and Mexicans have brought us a lot including richness of culture. I will comment that the Africans brought here in slavery, many were sold into it by their fellow Africans – a detail that is conveniently ignored by leftists and black activists. They were terribly treated but today we have another class that is being terribly exploited by the business leaders and the government, and the radical left is helping with this exploitation while claiming to be benevolent to them. These are the Central and South Americans who have come here illegally and without papers, mostly Mexican Illegal immigrants. I find them being here reprehensible, I believe in lawful immigration, but I also see the exploitation which is corollary to them being here as wrong. The radical left is abetting this by not working to get a reasonable immigration law that will allow them to come out of the shadows. Yes, I am opposed to illegal immigration, but I believe there is a reasonable solution somewhere out there between totally ending immigration, the current untenable situation and flying them in on cheese, steak and wine flights. It will take the ultra-conservatives and the radical left in congress getting their act together. It may not happen in my grandchildren's lifetime. We will not end this exploitation till this unholy alliance of the left and the exploiters is defeated.

Unlike the radical left, I consider the American culture one of the richest in the world, if not the richest. It has taken so much of the best of so many other cultures as people came, integrated with us and the best of their life was merged. It was partially assimilation and partly a modification of American Culture. We did not always appreciate these immigrants as much as we should have but we saw good in their culture and it became part of us. It would be well for current immigrants to recognize, they may not be immediately accepted or appreciated. Sometimes we modified parts of their culture in the process of adoption. Much of the ethnic foods we have adopted were modified enough that they are not recognized by those from that country, but they produced something good.

There is a joke that we had the choice of French cuisine, German engineering and British diplomacy and we took French engineering, German diplomacy and British cuisine, the worst of the lot. I really don't believe that, but it is funny. It does show how we adopted from others. I am not against any enrichment of our culture, in fact I welcome it but when a group tries to bring something in that is not wholesome, like the Muslim mistreatment of women and the desire to implement the hateful Sharia Law I say, "Stop." I will admit we have problems with women being treated with less than equality in our society. Check liberals like John Edwards, Harry Weinstein and Al Franken.[45] We do not need to bring in another cultural norm that

---

[45] As I write this, I find there is one conservative, Roy Moore and one RINO, GHW Bush, and a gaggle of lefties including Franken, a bunch of entertainment members and some news reporters. Two Republicans and all of these lefties

expands that. If Muslims want to come fine. Just drop that hateful system and ideas into the Atlantic on the way here. If you want to become a part of us you are welcome, that baggage is not. If you wish to worship that hateful God, Allah, fine. Just don't bring the things that violate US Law. Our legal system is imperfect. It is still head and shoulders above Sharia except in the minds of Islamic males who have a mental illness, Islam.

The concept of Saudi Law being to protect women is not even a myth, it is a barefaced lie.

The alt-Left – A pseudo-government

Although relatively new, the alt-left, particularly movements like Occupy, Black Lives Matter, and antifa claim to be for the working man, for the little guy but their power has come from various tactics that take away the rights of others. They apparently have heavy duty funding from the radical left. That funding is from people who would be decried as being in the 1% were it not for their support for left wing causes. You can be excused for exploitation if you give to left wing candidates and causes. There is strong evidence that the strong-armed mob protection rackets are back and are financing this hate filled uprising. The national media is avoiding mentioning this.

At Charlottsville the alt-left in the name of antifa confronted a white nationalist group. Damn the white nationalist group to hell for their policies if you like, I will too, but Antifa came, armed, body armor, and in riot mode, looking for a fight. They outnumbered the white group, possibly as much as 50 to 1. Many of the people they attracted were local, mostly good people but with the right environment and coaching, things can turn bad with only a few riot leaders in the group. A loud noise can set of a chain reaction. Mobs can be directed by a few. Common sense would have let that right-wing group march, let them get it out of their system and slink home but like oppressive governments the radical left allows no counter opinions, no dissent. Anyone who disagrees with them is to be silenced. It is like the Viet

---

are under scrutiny for abusing women. This is dealt with elsewhere. As of March 2018 the number in the entertainment industry, all lefties tops 30.

Cong and other repressive governments and hate movements like the Nazi one in Germany. To that end they played off old fears, hatreds and offenses to drag even well-meaning local blacks to gather, under their direction was a mob that was illegally there, and in numbers far beyond the ability of the police to handle, partially because the police were not coordinated and did not act soon enough. You must break up a mob before it gets too large to handle.

I have no part in white nationalist groups. I left a meeting one night in Hanover, PA because a speaker started an anti-sematic rant. Had it been anti-black, anti-Hispanic, anti- Italian hate rhetoric (you get it) I would have left. Had I known he or some other hate monger was on the docket; I would not have gone. I will not lend my support, good name or even my presence to such. Had I the opportunity to refute him, I would have taken it. But they have the right to free speech and expression and the marches and rants expose their evil even more. All but the most deranged can see it for what it is. Like that night in Hanover, I do not have to stay and listen. Generally, it is best to let them vent with an audience that could fit in a phone booth. The radical left at Charlottsville provided an audience and national exposure. They got more of that because of the Antifa led riot. The riot only served to gain sympathy for the white nationalists.

And there is another element here that needs to be mentioned. When the white nationalists hold a demonstration the funding for it is generally from within. They do not get funding from businesses, philanthropists, or even a general public support, a.k.a. tax money. As much as I hate to say it, this is the essence of democracy. I put my money where my mouth is.

When we look at the left-wing demonstrations, even the equipment that is available to them points to heavy duty funding. That money comes from somewhere. Many of these are 20 year old's living with their parents. One so-called grass roots demonstration being planned to protest gun violence in the wake of the Florida school shooting and started by students now has about 4 million dollars, some of it from Planned Parenthood that gets tax money. The left picks and choses what parts of the constitution are convenient to observe. They will use their right to assembly to step on the right to bear arms and even on another group's right to assembly as anti-fa did in Charlottsville. They have used their right to assembly and the right to redress to attack freedom of religion which appears in the same amendment of the Bill of Rights that the rights to assemble and redress appear. They can even split which parts of articles they will observe.

When John Ashcroft was being confirmed as Attorney General Teddy Kennedy violated Article VI of the constitution[46] by asking him if with his Assembly of God membership, could he uphold the constitution. Article VI clearly says no religious test is valid for any office in the US. But Kennedy, being from the left was above the law.

Enter Antifa with an evil political agenda of their own, one that is not better than the one they supposedly opposed. They wish to silence any speech or expression that does not meet their standards which are far from being as pure as the snow. The white supremists clearly advocate the violation of Amendment 14 but the left violates at least the first and want to abridge the second. They came to Charlottsville with weapons and with the idea of a confrontation with the white group and they got it. They came and accumulated numbers that were intended to either demoralize the whites or physically push them off the field. The city failed, either by not having enough resources, not deploying them properly or by design to keep the two groups separated. I would hate to believe they did it on purpose, but a case could be made that they allowed the confrontation that ultimately resulted in a death. If I were the family of the dead girl, I would be filing a wrongful death suit against the Antifa, Charlottsville police, the Virginia State Police and city government. I would not bother with the White Supremists for several reasons, they have no money and other than the one person who drove the car, they can argue with some validity that they had nothing in it. The others are not as well protected.

---

[46] The Senators and Representatives before mentioned, and the Members of the several State Legislatures, and all executive and judicial Officers, both of the United States and of the several States, shall be bound by Oath or Affirmation, to support this Constitution; but no religious Test shall ever be required as a Qualification to any Office or public Trust under the United States.

I have read the 'independent report' created at the request of the city. On page 18 (of about 80) it makes this statement.

> The City also protected the free expression of the Klan, despite its odious character. The City's response to the Klan event adequately accommodated both compelling interests at stake on July 8—free speech and public safety

July 8 was the precursor of the other event that resulted in deaths. This 'independent' report fails the objectivity litmus test with one phrase here describing the KKK; "despite its odious character". The character of speech, other than "crying fire in a crowded theatre" is not significant nor should it have been mentioned in a report that was to be objective. The writers of the report showed their bias in this statement. Antifa has the right to its vile speech and so does the KKK. What Antifa and the Klan do not have the right to is to intimidate and threaten. Even in the biased report there is no indication of such action by the Klan as a group. The death of the girl is the result of an individual, not the group. On the day of the death, there was a lot of blame to go around. The KKK could have called it off, but remember, they had a permit to hold the rally, they had dotted the I's and crossed the T's. They had paid for permits. Their numbers were well within the law, about half of what they had stated when applying for the permit. They altered plans as suggested by the city. They had stayed in the designated areas.

Antifa and other left-wing groups had called for a demonstration using social media, they did not have a permit, their numbers exceeded the city rules for assembly without a permit, long before the violence broke out. The city police, state police and other law enforcement failed to even attempt to disperse a crowd that had grown well past legal size. Antifa came with weapons and shields. To blame this on the KKK is like blaming the death of a pedestrian, run down while crossing legally in a crosswalk on another pedestrian in the crosswalk because he was there.

The confrontation occurred, it escalated to violence, Antifa against the police and the violence escalated till a white nationalist in frustration drove a car into a crowd, killing one young woman. I am not in any way condoning the act that resulted in her death but let us look at this from a very pragmatic view. She joined forces with a group bent on violence.

Whether or not she was a combatant she had willingly taken to the battlefield and was at risk to be harmed. She ignored the battle stance that Antifa had taken, either by design or stupidity. Had I been there and seen what was happening it would have been, get out of Dodge before the action. The police had set up two lines of barricades some yards apart to keep the two groups separate, a very prudent act. Unfortunately, these were the pipe barricades that look like bicycle racks and they were easily breached and opened by Antifa. They broke into the DMZ and advanced with weapons on the Klan. The Klan stayed behind their barricade. The police were ineffective in getting Antifa behind the barricades. This was mainly because the numbers had been allowed to grow to where the police did not have the resources to handle it. To their credit, the Klan did not go violent at the barricades. They had firearms but did not unshoulder them. This is in the report that blames the Klan. I must say, the Klan showed more restraint than I would have expected.

Certainly, the guy who drove the car must be taken to task and he needs to be severely punished, but anyone who did things to escalate the level of violence or allow it to escalate that day must bear blame at least as accessories before the fact. Antifa and the other counter demonstrators, as Donald Trump stated in another way, must bear some of the blame. It is easy to paint white nationalists as evil, but it seems that liberals, including most of the press can give a left-wing group that promotes violence a pass! What is not mentioned, Antifa came prepared to fight. They came in battle gear with weapons. They precipitated the fight and in fact the Klan backed away from the fight. Let me be clear here, I would not have supported their using gunfire to stop Antifa, but they backed away in spite of them being armed and attacked. Clearly, the Klan as a group wanted to avoid violence. They came to present their case, not riot. The Klan is despicable, but there is no indication that they precipitated that fight or contributed to it in any way other than by their presence which is their constitutional right, a right that is guaranteed to any group, the Klan or Antifa. The radical and violent left wing used violence to attempt to take away that right. The press has ignored that. It is one of the most visible examples of left-wing media bias.

In the report it is clear, the city failed to provide proper security at and in the zone around the demonstration. The intersection that could have stopped the speeding car was staffed by a police evidence person, a good person, a sworn officer, but without proper training for the post, unarmed, without proper support when she was threatened and called for support, without proper barricades (they were wooden saw horses), and after two attempts to get support she advised it was too risky to stay, and she had wisely withdrawn for her safety before the car passed the point. Had she been there her life would have been at risk and she had nothing to stop the car. She was not an armed officer. Remember, the demonstrators who caused her to fear for her life and withdraw were not Klan, they were counter demonstrators, i.e. Antifa and fellow travelers. Even if she had been there, she had the authority to stop the car but lacked, because of city and police leadership misfeasance, (possibly malfeasance) the means to stop it. <u>The city failed miserably in its basic duty, to provide for public and employee safety.</u> When planning for the event there was a request for cement barricades at that intersection, it was nixed. The threat was seen in the planning and the threat ignored. Again, a lawsuit for the woman's death is in order. When the officer retreated, and I agree with her action which she properly reported as she was leaving the post, only three wooden sawhorses guarded the intersection and the critical one was subsequently moved out of place. It would not have stopped a speeding car, it would have only served to protect if the person driving the car honored the traffic control it provided or it somehow disabled the car, an unlikely expectation. To blame the Klan for that death was totally unfounded. Yes, the blame is on the one individual, but others abetted him. But it gets better or should I say worse. The report also blames the deaths of the two officers in a State Police helicopter crash nearby on the Klan! That is some stretch! I have seen no indication, not even a fake news allegation that the Klan shot down that bird or contributed in any way to the crash.

Antifa was there that day to silence dissenting speech. No matter how reprehensible that speech, and it is, it is still allowed under the constitution unless it hits certain levels and that is for the courts to decide, not an armed group of Antifa thugs on the street. They were no better than the white nationalists they opposed, and in fact if you look at motives, the white nationalists had the moral high ground. The Klan members were there to exercise their constitutional right to free speech. They had jumped through the legal hoops to get a permit to be there and they were many and every legal hurdle was used to prevent the demonstration. Antifa was there to deny them that right, a right granted by the constitution and affirmed by the city and state when they issued the permit. No, I do not agree with the white nationalist line. But they have the right to present it. When we have someone, the government, the courts, the social media moguls, the thugs in the street, or even me, no matter which, deciding what speech is valid, we no longer have free speech. Certainly, there is a level at which speech must be limited, speech that advocates violence for example and that is usually over the line far enough that reasonable people will agree it need be throttled.

When I see the masked Antifa I am reminded of another socialist left-wing group that took power by intimidation and threats. It was in Germany in the 1930's when the Nazi party took power! I consider this group and their fellow travelers as dangerous as Adolf Hitler and his followers.

I have some mixed feelings on a group needing a permit to gather. It is a slippery slope for government to control free speech. Sure, it is a local government with limited reach, but it still is the government with the ability to imprison or fine. On the other hand, as a member of an Emergency Operations Center, I see the reason and need for the permit to help us prepare for the event. In looking at the laws and how Charlottsville handled this I see real constitutional violations. They worked hard to allow the free speech demonstration but failed to ensure the safety and as an aside, the Klan made some concessions to help the city insure safety.

Unfortunately, Charlottsville dropped a couple balls in the planning. I will straddle the fence here, the requests should almost never be rejected or even modified unless there is a significant risk to the public safety that **cannot be mitigated**, and then, accommodations should be aggressively sought. If a group were going to shut down a critical highway, the city should work to find a different location that would serve their purpose, maybe the walk way of a bridge that spans it and limit the numbers to so there is safety for the public and the demonstrators. If the day is bad because of some other event, etc. see if an acceptable alternate date or limiting the time can be used. The idea that a government agency can shut down dissent causes me to shudder but if all good faith attempts at reasonable mitigation fail, I can accept it.

Black Lives Matter, another left-wing organization and a fellow traveler with the Antifa is no better. Much of their rhetoric is based on lies, just plain out and out fabrications. It is good at getting someone judged in the press that is increasingly hostile to whites, police and guns. The "hands up don't shoot" it took as its slogan turned out to be false as judged by even some left-wing papers[47] however the coverage of the truth got little attention, little ink and nearly zero air time. The St. Louis Rams players,[48] wide receiver Stedman Bailey (12) and wide receiver Tavon Austin (11) and tight end Jared Cook (89) and wide receiver Chris Givens (13) and wide receiver Kenny Britt (81) put their hands up to show support for Michael Brown before a game against the Oakland Raiders at the Edward Jones Dome. (USA Today Sports via Reuters) in another display of idiocy when they entered the field. With this support for an idea, it has to be true. The average NFL fan doesn't read the news one week later when it is correctly reported. The celebrity carries the message.

I might add that many of those who spout that line have armed bodyguards. If the officer is white and the perp is black, when the perp gets perforated with a bullet, the officer is automatically a racist. Yes, there have been police who have gone over the edge and should have been disciplined, removed from the force and some jailed for actions against citizens of any color. But they are few and quite frankly, many of them happen in cities where the police have been under left wing Mayors and City Councils for decades and they have neglected their duty to weed out bad officers. It is a chain of malfeasance in office that has brought is to this and it is driven by malfeasance in the voting booth

---

[47] https://www.washingtonpost.com/news/fact-checker/wp/2015/03/19/hands-up-dont-shoot-did-not-happen-in-ferguson/
[48] https://www.nbcnews.com/storyline/michael-brown-shooting/rams-players-enter-field-hands-dont-shoot-pose-n258561

when the people continue to elect the same people. Why when we have politicians promise to clean up police forces, which many of these did on multiple times, do the police forces still have the rotten apples? More pointedly, if the public really cares about this, why do they keep electing them? The answer is easy, the lie the Democrats have told, we are the only ones who care about minorities, it widely believed.

These left-wing politicians have bowed to unions that contribute to political campaigns. These officials should bear the weight of the law with the errant officer. The Christophers had a TV program, it began, "It is better to light one candle than to curse the darkness." I would like to say to these mayors and city councils, "It is better to do your job effectively than make political speeches." Many of these cities have and have had for decades, Democrat mayors, some black. Many of those police forces have black chiefs and have not aggressively worked to weed out the rotten apples, even white rotten apples! Why not? Where are the leaders in this? If these white racist officers are still on the force, why are they there? The city governments, not the thugs on the street, should be acting. I would not expect a newly elected mayor to turn it around in a month, but in his second or third term, it should be getting better. The officer who choked the man in NYC probably should have been placed on permanent desk duty for policy violations years before the incident and I have no problem with moving a person who has exhibited behavior that indicates his or her presence on the street with a badge is not prudent to another job, temporarily or permanently. But he was on the street for years with a bad record. I am not sure if he was a racist, but by all appearances he certainly went beyond what was good enforcement and had a history for excess. You don't have to be white or a racist to exceed your authority. I cannot with certainty say this act was racist. It did exceed his authority. It is possible this guy was also just a victim of the pressures of the job, but that is no reason to either let him there or put him out on the street. Look for a place to use the skills he has, safely.

But without any equivocation I ask, "With his record, and it was bad, why was he still on the street?" It is far easier to judge the act, exceeding the authority, than the alleged motivation, racism. The former is sufficient to weed out bad officers, the latter winds up in a urinating contest and feeds hatred in the street without fixing the problem. But most mayors and police chiefs are afraid of the unions or in league with them. The fear if the closing the tap of union money for campaigns. Can we call them what they are, bribes?

Look at the outcome of the Freddie Grey and Michael Brown sagas. Most of the officers were exonerated and in the Michael Brown case, the officer was additionally cleared by the Federal Justice Department under no other than Loretta Lynch. Even the biased left listing DC 'lynch mob' couldn't find something to charge him with. I am sure had there been one single shred of evidence the officer did something wrong including littering, he would have been Lynched by Loretta Lynch and the Justice Department. I am surprised that he was not accused of littering. His weapon ejected cartridge cases as he fired. If he didn't pick up the brass, why wasn't he charged with littering for the spent brass or the dead thug he left on the street as he was taken to the hospital for treatment of his injuries? That was a 6 foot 200 plus pound thug stretched out on the street, not the 14 year-old cherub with headphones that was pictured on TV.

Michael Brown was a thug who robbed a store, strong arm, tried to take a cop's gun, assaulted the cop and placed the cop in enough fear for his life when he shot the thug. I am darned sure that the 'hands up, don't shoot' was a lie. Why? Easy. If he had his hands up, I am sure there were people there videoing it and it would have been presented to the press had it been supportive of the agenda. I bet there is video out there that would substantiate the officer's statement that Brown didn't have his hands up. I would love to see a reward of $25,000 be offered for video that shows it. I am sure that would smoke it out. I will add that the officer's statement does not conflict with physical evidence in any way and in fact most of his story is solidly supported by the evidence. He is a credible witness. BLM seized on the 'hands up don't shoot' lie and even when it was well proven to be false, BLM still hangs on that. A lie is a lie. Repeating it as truth makes you a liar. The bands of liars still walk the street yelling 'hands up don't shoot' and raising their hands. It is an emotional rallying point that the dishonest, uneducated, stupid and emotional can rally around. With the left, rational thought is replaced by emotion and rhetoric. Like the Borg Collective of Star Trek, everyone must think alike.

Woodrow Wilson

NEGRO FEDERAL OFFICERS.
No negroes are now left in important federal positions in the south, although ten years ago there were a number holding places of responsibility, with attractive salaries. Dr. D. A. Crum as collector of customs at Charleston and J. W. Rucker, as collector of internal revenue at Atlanta were among the last removed from office. At the beginning of this fiscal year, July 1, other negroes were removed from minor federal positions and their offices given to men of the white race.

The 'great progressive' and globalist Woodrow Wilson came to the White House in 1913. Together the two words translate to socialist. Much negative has been written about the Reconstruction period after the Civil War, most by leftists and southerners who were not allowed to continue the oppression of blacks during that time. It was not all bad. It was necessary to wrest the power from those who had engaged in the fight to continue slavery, albeit on a new kind of plantation. I doubt that those who wrote those laws had any idea the difficulty of the process and how ingrained was the enemy, the southern Aristocrat. Harsh measures were needed to break the chains of slavery, much to end the domination by the white aristocracy. The reconstruction laws did that and I might add, quite effectively but too often medicine is stopped before it fully cures the illness.   When that happens, the infection comes roaring back and it did starting in the 1890's. Reconstruction ended and the whites started heading blacks back to the plantation. Slavery was out, but a neo-slavery was instituted.

During the 1865-1900 period blacks in both the south and north gained a lot of freedom. Blacks were elected to both state and federal legislatures. All was not great, but many things were headed in a positive direction. The tide was turning against blacks in the south as the children and grandchildren of the aristocracy grabbed the reins of government. And then along came Woodrow. The day Wilson came to power there were a significant number of blacks in the US government. How many of them he fired shortly after his inauguration varies depending on source, from all to only those with positions of influence. The number fired would be reprehensible even it was only one because his reason was so deplorable that I wonder why his statues are not being torn down along with those of Robert E. Lee and Jeff Davis. I forgot, he was a left leaning, liberal, progressive Democrat. That whitewashes him. He said blacks were not capable of leadership and

OSBORNE CONFIRMED.

Col. W. M. Lassiter Urged for Promotion to Rank of Brigadier
General, United States Army.

Observer Bureau,
297 Hibbs Building,
Washington, April 24.

President Wilson today replaced
two more negro Federal officeholders
with white men, this answering the
query as to whether he would let
his Virginia blood or New Jersey
training guide him in appointments.
The positions for which he nominated
white men today pay $5,000 each.

Samuel J. Graham of Pennsylvania
was nominated as Assistant Attorney
General, to succeed William H. Lewis. The latter was Attorney General
Wickersham's assistant, for whom he
made a vigorous fight to retain in the
American Bar Association.

Edward Luck, now of Wisconsin,
was nominated as Auditor of the
Navy Department. This place is now
filled by Ralph Tyler of Ohio, who is
a negro. This change will be deeply
gratifying to naval officers, as in the
past they have been forced to go to
Tyler and explain their accounts and
secure his approval.

In this office are a number of other
negro clerks. One of them is Pe-
kney, the barber to former President
Roosevelt, who is listed as an accountant.

hence had no place in the government. Really? Tell me what would happen if Donald Trump made that statement. What if it was learned that Regan had said that? How about Ike or GWB? But the alt-left will excuse and hide Wilson's action because he was a liberal, progressive Democrat. Use of the word progressive to describe Wilson taints the word. The article shown from the Charlotte Observer April 25, 1913

VIRGINIA BLOOD SEEMS UPPERMOST

President Wilson Replaced Two Negro Officeholders With White Men.

NEGRO FEDERAL OFFICERS.

No negroes are now left in important federal positions in the south, although ten years ago there were a number holding places of responsibility, with attractive salaries. Dr. D. A. Crum as collector of customs at Charleston and J. W. Rucker, as collector of internal revenue at Atlanta were among the last removed from office. At the beginning of this fiscal year, July 1, other negroes were removed from minor federal positions and their offices given to men of the white race.

Page1 (Newspapers.com)

details how two black government workers, Ralph Tyler and William H. Lewis were replaced. Lewis was the Assistant Attorney General. Lewis's previous boss made an appeal to keep him, certainly an indication his performance was not an issue. It was his skin color. Whites would have the indignity (not my wording – Wilsons.) of having to go to a black man for approval! The article says that many of the naval officers were gratified that Tyler was leaving as they had to go to him for approval of and explain their accounts. Is it possible that he was just doing his job well? Here is another example from Charlotte Observer April 29, 1913 Page1. (Newspapers.com) There is no explanation of this comment, so I am left to believe it was demeaning to have to explain their accounts to a 'negro' who was in their minds below them because of his skin color.

At one point I was considering this may have been an isolated incident that was being blown out of proportion. But look at the two portions of an article from the Daily Ardimoriete (Ardmore OK) July 6, 1913, a few months later. It details how many officers were removed. If you read on you will learn that it is not a bash of these men being removed but a blast against these men who were characterized as lazy and not fulfilling their jobs! It was the standard Dixie evil rhetoric of the lazy black and it got to the place where Wilson was simply systematically removing blacks.

Unfortunately, this lie and the one that blacks only want to have sex with white women have survived the Confederacy and Dixie eras. I deal with this lie in the section, "The Confederacy." By the time Wilson's presidency was six months old, blacks were having a hard time. Also note that the previous Republican administration is accused of championing the 'negro' cause.[49] In an April 22, 1913 cabinet meeting Wilson broke from his promise in the campaign to "treat negros fairly" and said he did not make any real promise. Wilson won that election by the large number of blacks who had previously voted Republican and voted for him. This began the federal segregation that included the postal workers. Many blacks lost their jobs and they had voted for the man who made it happen.

Those who demonize Republicans on civil rights should remember Lincoln's emancipation proclamation, Ev Dirkson's work to get the Civil Rights bill passed and Eisenhower's orders to integrate schools and colleges. At Ike's direction Federal Troops with M-1's faced state troopers. No Democrat including Barak Obama, FDR, WJC and certainly Woodrow Wilson have the credentials to stand with these men in guarding the rights of all Americans, including those of color. See, when the rights of one is preserved, it strengthens the rights of all. When the rights of one is diminished, the rights of all are likewise.

Blacks had already shown their ability to lead, holding positions in State and Federal Legislatures and responsible positions in the government. When reconstruction ended, and the White (Democrat) Aristocracy was able to wrest control back into their hands, organize squads to suppress blacks and the black vote, pass laws restricting rights of blacks including voting and public access, form the KKK, and take the right to have weapons from blacks; things were in the white aristocracy terms, normalizing. And they were very proud of it. Note the political party of the delegation sent to congress.

> The state that up to a few years ago sent negro congressmen to the national house of representatives now enjoys with Louisiana and Mississippi the distinction of a solid democratic delegation in the national congress.

The Semi-Weekly Messenger Wilmington NC 22 nov 1898

[49] https://postalmuseum.si.edu/research-articles/the-history-and-experience-of-african-americans-in-america%E2%80%99s-postal-service-3

Think about that when you hear those who will confiscate guns. That was done with blacks by laws in the south and it allowed KKK gangs to run roughshod over blacks. Imagine this scene. A group of thirty white hooded KKK arrive at the home of a black who has been too vocal. The object, burn a cross, show him who is in charge, maybe even drag him out of the house and beat or kill him. They light the cross and a couple of shots go over the heads of the cross burners or maybe a round hits the leader's chest and he starts leaking blood. I smile when I think of the physical impact on his chest and the emotional one on the others. I assure you that would dampen the enthusiasm for burning crosses. It is irony that the much-maligned NRA, yes the National Rifle Association was the only organization that opposed those laws that prevented blacks from owning weapons! The laws of prohibiting blacks from owning weapons dates back to 1640 but really geared up in the era after the Civil War. [50] It included the "Black Codes."

When reconstruction ended the southern whites, who were previously prevented from being in government because of their involvement in the rebellion were 'white washed', they and their children entered the political arena and able to go back to their old ways. Slavery was out but the neo-slavery was in. Blacks were back on the virtual plantation. And Wilson removed some of the remaining influence blacks were making in the government. It is things like this that the idiot firebrands today use to show blacks how they have been disadvantaged and worse, many of them are willing to live in the past, not the present where many of the barriers have been removed in spite of the Democrats in the South, the US Senate, the House and the White House. I will discuss this in the section, "Early Twentieth Century Dixie." Many Democrats in the 1960's – even from the north were not champions of civil rights.

But Wilson participated in another and even far greater oppressive act against all Americans with his creation of the Committee on Public Information when the war started. He oppressed blacks, sure, but he also oppressed whites! Immigrants including citizens were targeted based on national origin. This organization, formed in April 1917 was

---

[50] https://www.theatlantavoice.com/articles/gun-control-historically-has-meant-prohibiting-blacks-from-owning-one/

also called the Creel Committee for George Edward Creel who lead it. One of its big lies was painting the draft as selecting the best, the ones the government needed. It was done by changing the name to Selective Service, you were the one selected to save America. It was actually collecting fodder to feed to the hogs of war. It is interesting to me that when I registered for 'Selective Service' in 1962, nearly 50 years after Creel, it had a sign 'Selective Service Board' but I can't ever remember it being called anything but the draft board. It is harder to fool the average citizen than the politicians think.

Wilson looked back at the draft riots in the War of the Rebellion in 1861 and decided there must be a way to prevent that. To that end the lie of conscripts being special was concocted. Once you start lying you find it easy to keep doing it. More lies and half-truths were concocted, and George Creel became adept at leading a propaganda system that quickly morphed to one who had no concerns about truth and the constitutional rights of citizens. After all, a half truth is still a lie, but it is far more credible because it is half true. Many will believe the whole thing when they fail to see the crap imbedded in the truth. "A spoonful of sugar makes the medicine go down."[51] Nancy Pelosi recently said, "They handed us a cup of poop with a cherry and called it a Sundae." It was a Republican written bill and she would have said that had it been ice cream. That is exactly what Wilson's propaganda arm handed the public. The cherry was the promise of safety in a world gone mad with war. The poop was anything that would convince Americans to support his war effort. To ensure action, you need to create a boogeyman. The southern aristocrats created the sex crazed black man who wanted only to rape your wife and daughters. Hitler talked about international Jewry. Creel created his boogeyman, American citizens of German and Australian descent. It stated that these descendants were possibly the enemy, a trojan horse in America and got to the point that it was not only possible, they were. Maybe these American citizens had loyalties to their homeland. Although nothing of the sort was proven this concept was beaten into the minds of Americans by Creel. That they could have sympathies for their homeland, activate and commit acts of sabotage is also possible. So far what we have said is the truth. This all

---

[51] Spoonful of Sugar is a song from The Sound of Music

could be. But the CPI focused on this including comments that if your neighbor was of German or Austrian origin; if they had an ethnic name like Brandt, Fenstermacher, Geiger, Falkenstine; they were to be watched, they may be disloyal, they may be a saboteur. They may be plotting to kill loyal Americans in their beds. They may be planning to blow up factories, railroads and public buildings. They probably are. Even those of German descent were often suspicions of those who came later. If they had German festivals, spoke German, read a German Newspaper, etc. they may be plotting sabotage.[52] All of this is true. They could be. But should they be watched and kept in line? These were for the most part loyal Americans who were demonized and even most who were not loyal were not bent to act against the nation. Most were just thankful for the right to be here, not in war torn Europe. Most had left hardship behind for a better life. The ties to the homeland were weak.

German had been a popular foreign language in schools, in fact the most taught foreign language in 1914. This almost ended in this time. Anything German was not loyal. Please note, the English-Spanish language mix we have today is not new. In 1914 many Americans spoke German, some as a first language. The language spoken in many homes was German, but few were not conversant in English. Suddenly newspapers stopped printing German editions. Those of German and Austrian origin tried to distance themselves from their heritage to the extent that many changed the spelling of their names. Our family did not, hence the name still has the German spelling, Brandt, not the English Brant, Brand or Brent. Let me make it personal. My grandparents quit speaking German around home during that time. The home was originally bi-lingual. My dad was born in 1912. He was five at the time the first world war started and knew little German because use of it was stopped at home. I might have had that heritage had this not happened. I might not have struggled through German in college. Without Wilson's propaganda blitzkrieg I might have had it easier. Worse than this small impact on me, the hysteria was whipped to a fever pitch. Cartoons and slogans painted anything German as evil.

---

[52] There was a weekly German language newspaper published in York PA into the early 1900's.

Creel cartoons depicted Germans with contorted faces. There were similar initiatives on Austrian origin, but the main thrust was against anything and anyone German. People were pulled out of their homes and beaten, more than a few killed, some were imprisoned, because they 'looked disloyal'. All it took in some areas was someone with a German name not seeming to be totally supporting the war effort. A simple statement that questioned the war could be a reason to be suspect. Over 13,000 were imprisoned under suspicion. Some were still being held a year after the war. There was only one significant on-shore event that may have been sabotage, the Black Tom explosion. Although sabotage is the official determination of the event it is also possible that was caused by careless storage and handling of explosives. Just the size of the explosion, the quantity of explosives unwisely stored in close proximity screams, "careless storage." It would not be either the first or last time such an event was carelessness. The final result was to blame a German Saboteur, and that is likely, but common sense tells me the explosion would not have been as bad had reasonable storage practices been used. CPI used this event to demonize those of German ancestry and it drove some hellish things including violence.

Wilson's policy forever changed America. There has been some revival of German language and culture in the US, but it has taken many years. It is likely that World War II slowed the revival. Like the Japanese and Chinese mentioned earlier, the German immigrants brought some significant good things to the American Culture. Go to Lancaster County PA (and other counties near it) where the culture has somewhat survived. You can go to restaurants that feature German cuisine, admittedly a heavy diet, but so good. I joke that at one of the buffet restaurants they should provide fork trucks to get you to the car. But there is much more than that. The German work ethic, the mechanical and farm expertise, the commitment to family and community have made south central PA a great place to live. Fifty years ago, in York PA, a German immigrant conclave, we cut iron parts, printed books and baked cookies. Nearly every major industry either did these or supported these. Packaged ice cream started in York County when dairy farms were producing too much milk, a problem, that was solved by turning in it into ice cream and shipping it to nearby cities, requiring refrigerated rail cars for shipment and heavy static refrigeration to produce it. These were 'problems' that York Countians and those around them solved. A joke at Caterpillar referred to the 'dumb Dutchmen' in the York Plant. They were dumb. In many cases they were too dumb to know that something couldn't be done so they went ahead and did it while the engineers were writing reports of the impossibility. They were not supermen, just creative and determined. They could absorb repeated failure and try again. It exists in many cultures, but my experience shows the Germans fine-tuned it. I am going to throw in this as balance. I have worked with Hispanics, they have fantastic historic and current work ethic. They will just do it. Their background talks of a mid-day siesta, it is not laziness, it is a very sensible and wise thing in the hotter places they previously lived. The Orientals I have known typically have patience, way beyond mine. The statement in 'The Karate Kid', 'Man who catches flies with chopsticks can do anything' has rung true with the ones I have known. These traits are not universal in the group, this is not profiling but the people I have known from the backgrounds usually have those traits. I think is it more upbringing than innate. For the most part it is good if not taken to distraction.

Other cultures have enriched this and in some cases tempered some of the bad in that German culture. With many blacks, Hispanics, Greeks, Italians, Poles, Rumanians, Hungarians, and some I recognize only by the ethnicity of the names, we have a society here that is diverse, but let us face adversity and we come together and are a darned impressive force unless the politicians and rabble rousers get involved. Diversity is not our strength and never will be. Diverse backgrounds with unity of purpose is great strength. The York plan of World War II that mobilized American Industry to the war effort had its roots in this ethnic mix. Aid for flood or fire victims comes from every group without regard for who is flooded or burned out. A police officer, fire fighter, etc. is killed and there is an outpouring of caring and support for his family. Only the liberals protest. I guess their upbringing is deficient. It is interesting to watch this, the different cultures doing it in their own historic ways. But they do it. And the mixture is awesome. My only regret is we don't do it as effectively day to day. The German core here in York County is a part of that which has been seasoned and expanded with the various spices and contributions of the other groups. Like a good meal, the sum is far

greater than the parts. We have our problems. We could do far better.
But we have done a lot right and I see signs of improvement. As an
aside, the addition of the Hispanic, Oriental, Italian and Greek foods to
the mix are awesome. I will admit I avoid the heavily spiced ones but
when I can keep that to a reasonable level, I like the variety.

Several years ago, I was at an aid station at the Red Lion Street Fair
(southern York County PA). A group next to us was Philippine. Please
remember this is in the heart of a population that is mainly of German
descent. In the middle of the afternoon about a dozen very pretty
women from about 15 to 50 lined up along the sidewalk, music started,
and they sang two songs, first, 'The Star Spangled Banner' and then the
national anthem of their homeland. I was taken back in a couple ways.
I was unaware of this group even existed here and just as important,
their commitment to America and their heritage. Both are good if set in
the proper frame. I didn't recognize the second song but felt it was
important enough to stand with respect until they finished as many did.
I walked over, thanked them and asked, that is how I learned the song's
name. When I asked the one lady told me what the other song was and
said, "We are Americans, but we are from the Philippines." She has it
right. So did most Americans of German origin. They were Americans
from Germany. Creel needed a demon. He used the German heritage
here much like Hitler did the Jews in Germany. Both were wrong.

Yes, Germany and Austria were the enemy. But to consider Americans,
many of whom were here for long periods before the war as possible
terrorists and saboteurs was way over the top. Many left there to avoid
the wars. Many of their descendants with German names went to
Europe to end German oppression in 1917 and 1944 and all too many
did not come back. Nesbur Gilton Brandt, an uncle, was one of them.
He died April 15, 1945 in Northern Italy on Hill 905 attempting to rescue
his wounded platoon leader. He was on combat only 15 days and in the
elite 88th Mountain Division this 30 year-old guy from the backwoods of
Pennsylvania won the Infantry Badge – given to men who show they can
fight – and the Silver Star and Purple Heart.

I could have understood and would have suggested some scrutiny,
particularly for recent immigrants or if someone really looked disloyal
but not the Creel hysteria level. We should always be observant. I don't

care if my neighbor has a name of Mohammed, Abdul, Little Wolf, Hans, Willie, Harry, Juan, Win, or Charlie, if he starts doing things that could be threatening, I dial will 911. I may not be totally pure in this, I will admit, Mohammed or Abdul are likely to get a little more scrutiny, but the level on the 911 call is essentially the same. If it looks like a threat it is treated like a threat.

Let's put it into another perspective. Today we are at war with Islam. What would happen if we started rounding up and imprisoning anyone with an Arabic name or maybe dragging them out of their homes and beating them if their first name was Mohammed or Abdul? The same liberal conclaves that produced this program in World War I would have a cow. This is one place I would agree, I would too. CPI, Wilson's brainstorm, drove the hysteria that produced that with Germans. I would not be party to that.

Wilson oppressed those on the battlefield. World War I was fought in the trenches and in waves of men crossing no man's land. Much improved artillery shells and the introduction of the machine gun were devastating to the troops who were used with tactics from the 1700's. The absolute worst machine gun of the war was the French sho sho. It was so bad it should never have been deployed. The best machine guns on the battlefield were the British Vickers and the German guns but there was an awesome American weapon that was better than either of these. The measure of a machine gun is simple. How fast will it fire? Will it perform on battlefield conditions, ie. dirt. Will be able to sustain fire, i.e. not overheat. In other words, will it effectively deter or stop the enemy? To appease the French, Wilson bought sho sho's from the French to outfit the American Army. The propaganda story was we were afraid to have the American gun on the battlefield where the Germans could capture one and duplicate it. So American Soldiers died when the sho sho's jammed at critical times, the big negative of them. If they hadn't been prone to jamming in a dirty environment, they would still not have been in the league with the Vickers. They were bought to satisfy Wilson's diplomacy. We see after the war how bad it was.

The globalist Wilson failed to jam the League of Nations down the throats of various nations and failed to get the Congress to accept it.

That only delayed the implementation of it, albeit with a different name, The UN, for 30 years. I for one look at the UN as a negative force in the world. It has failed miserably to improve the lot of many and has created situations that are totally against any reason. It has also been a tool of oppressors. Like mobsters, they support one another when freedom and rights are at stake. Check the list of nations on the human rights panels in a later section.

FDR

The country was in the midst of the great depression when FDR came to power. He took the reins firmly and began driving the country toward the New Deal that was really socialism under another high-sounding name. A pile of poop is still a pile of poop even if you call it fertilizer or put a cherry on it and call it a sundae. The New Deal was a pile of stinky stuff much larger than the one in any barnyard. I look at the Green New Deal that is being touted by a failed college graduate who was working as a bar maid who became a member of the House or Representatives. Why would someone with a Masters in Business be working as a bar maid? I have listened to her speak. Had I interviewed her for a job requiring that background, I wouldn't have hired her. The phrase 'air head' comes to mind every time I hear her. She rarely produces a complete sentence.

Look at some of her key ideas. End air travel. Let us try that on the tourist industry, particularly the places like Florida and Hawaii. Without air travel the 2,400 miles from San Francisco to Hawaii is easily a 70 hour boat ride at 30 knots or 35 miles an hour. To get from New York to San Francisco by rail at sixty miles an hour is another 40 hours. Without air travel we have four and a half days of travel each way for a Hawaiian vacation. The roughly 5000 miles by air is under 12 hours. Do you think that would harm tourism? They have also signed on to UN Agenda 21 – a hellish document with a name "sustainability" to cover it. I have read it. It would move ownership of all land, vehicles and weapons to the state, if you needed one you would get "approval" and "rent" what the state thought you needed. If this sounds like communism to you, it is.

By early 1937 FDR's plans to drive the country into a socialist system were in serious jeopardy, the result of the Supreme Court following the law and striking most of his ideas as unconstitutional. With that backdrop on February 5, 1937[53] he announced a plan to appoint additional justices that were friendly to his policies. Most people if asked would say, the constitution says nine justices. Wrong. The constitution only specifies that there will be a Supreme Court and a Chief Justice with associate justices, the number nine is not specified. It could be a three or thirty person court. I am sure some who read this will not believe me and get a copy of the constitution and check because we have always had 9. FDR proposed a bill to provide retirements for justices at the age of 70 and if they chose not to retire an assistant with voting rights would be added at the president's appointment with a limit of 15 justices. Since the constitution did not specify the number of justices, no constitutional question could arise in this. The current justices could not constitutionally be pushed off the bench, but they could be neutralized by FDR appointed liberals. Justices can die on the bench with their robes on and we have one who may, hoping for a Trump free White House to appoint her successor. A few such appointments and his policies would be approved. He justified it by saying it would make the court more efficient but all Republicans and many Democrats in the congress opposed the plan. It was all about making the court an arm of the socialist movement in the United States. Fortunately, enough in congress saw the danger and refused to support the effort.

FDR had contempt for the court and it appears he had contempt for the constitution, not an unusual stance for a liberal. A true liberal, he knew what he wanted to do, he was the elite, he knew what was best for the country and why would anyone question him? That is the mantra of the communist system, we, the party, are the elite, we know what is best for the masses. He called the court, "Nine old men, sitting on the bench, making arbitrary decisions about something they know nothing." Obama's excoriation of the court in his State of the Union Address brought this to mind. I also remember the justice who mouthed, "lie." He had the right to mouth that, it is free speech, it was how he saw it, the press in their attempt to make an issue covered it. The press

---

condemned him but never addressed the accuracy of the Obama comment that was far from the truth.

Several events intervened to prevent this twisting of the court. First, two justices came to the liberal side and the court allowed the creation of the National Labor Relations Board and Social Security, two FDR sacred cows. There are questions about the validity and wisdom of Social Security, but they pale when compared to the NLRB that has been a scourge to the country since its founding and in fact bit FDR during the war by legitimizing the coal strikes. Second, the congress soundly defeated the measure to pack the court 70-22 in July and it died. FDR appointed his first justice in 1937 and by 1942 seven of the justices were his appointees. If this was Bill Clinton I would have had concerns he had the ex-Justices wacked or threatened but then, that was possible with FDR. His moral compass sometimes seemed to not have a magnetized needle. It is interesting to note that had the Twenty Second amendment of the constitution been in effect before 1940 FDR would not have been president in January 1941. The 22nd was ratified in 1951, just before Harry Truman could have been elected to a <u>second elected term</u>.

This is one place the founding fathers lacked foresight, not having term limits for congress, not just for the president but for the legislature too. But they never saw the politics as a profession. In their mind, who would want that? The answer is simple, the greedy and power drunk. Look at the rabble there today who have never had a job outside government. That is biting us in the rear now with 30 plus year congressmen and women who need to be retired. They have become professional politicians, something the founding fathers did not see. George Washington exercised term limits voluntarily and that held till we encountered an egomaniac who ran for terms three and four. With the 22nd, Truman was ineligible because he served more than two years of FDR's fourth term. Although FDR was elected four times, he served just over twelve years. Harry was FDR's third vice president, John N. Garner served from 1933 to 1941, Henry A. Wallace from 1941 to 1945 and Harry S. Truman from January 20, 1945 to April 12, 1945, less than 3 months.

I find it interesting to look at people and events and ask, "What if history were different?" As an aside I do that in two books, WW2 - An Alternate History and the D-Day landing has failed. What if the 22nd amendment had been delayed and not ratified till after the 1952 election and Harry had been elected for the third term, certainly a possibility. Stevenson was on the Democrat ticket only because they didn't have anyone else, behind Harry, the Democrats had no bench. Ike was popular but with the power of the incumbency Truman may have beaten Ike. His biggest liability was the firing of Douglas MacArthur – something that was not popular with many who adored the general, primarily because he had a good press agent, not his military ability. I personally rate him below every other American general in World War II and in the ranks with the lackluster ones from the Civil War. He had an ego as big as Patton without the ability to match. Looking at world Generals he would have been a good tie with Montgomery who I believe did more damage to the Allied cause than any two German Generals. In my opinion Doug was the best two Generals the Japanese had.

Now roll ahead a couple years to Old Miss and Little Rock. Would Harry, who I respect, but a Democrat who had to work with the Dixiecrats, have taken the decisive actions Ike, a Republican did, of Federal troops and marshals forcibly integrating these institutions? I will answer it this way. I have studied Harry, consider him one of the greater presidents, but I consider it a 50-50 crap shoot at best. I have great respect for Harry, but I cannot find a statement from him of support or the opposite on these moves. One thing I respect about Harry, when he was an ex-president, he was out of the public eye.

Of the presidents in my lifetime, I only consider two would have been likely to do it, Regan and Obama. For Regan it would have been an act of courage as it was with Ike. Obama would have done what would have been the right thing, but it would have been a despicable act because it would have been done to spite 'whitey', not to benefit blacks. I believe Ike reached back into his past, saw blacks as equals, saw their contribution to winning the war and with a man of the caliber of Ike, it doesn't matter what flack comes, it is the right thing to do. He was like Farragut at Mobile Bay, "Damn the torpedoes, full speed ahead."[54] I base this on the character of this man as the commander of Allied forces in Europe, dealing with the intense ego of Bernard Montgomery who more than a few times made statements to Ike and the press that Ike was not capable of handling the job, only Montgomery could do that. Let us just say Monty's battleship mouth was bigger than his row-boat ability. Although many see Patton as the egomaniac, he recognized Ike for his strengths, sometimes fumed with Ike's decisions, but respected him as his superior officer and as a man. If George Patton had an ego the size of a large hill in Pennsylvania, Monty had one the size of Everest. Ike understood humility. If you doubt this, check the note Ike wrote to be read if the D-Day landing failed – and Monty, not Ike was the planner. The caliber of the man shows through, something I did not completely see until I was researching the novel, "The D-Day Landing Has Failed." My respect for Ike has soared since I read this.

> "Our landings in the Cherbourg-Havre area have failed to gain a satisfactory foothold and I have withdrawn the troops. My decision to attack at this time and place was based upon the best information available. The troops, the air and the navy did all that bravery and devotion to duty could do. If any blame or fault attaches to the attempt, it is mine alone."

Also check Monty's other big plan, Market Garden, and the number of lives that were lost because it was 'A Bridge Too Far'. It was Monty's attempt at self-glory.   It cost lives and did not achieve the objective. The movie of it is quite accurate.

Garner split with FDR in 1937 over several issues and in fact ran a primary campaign and sought the presidency in 1940. Garner, a

---

[54] At Mobile Bay the Confederacy had placed floating mines, they were called torpedoes then, in the bay. They could sink a ship if hit. The ship commanders wanted to steer clear of them but that would have been to make slow speed. It would also have placed them in the range of shore batteries for longer and made them easier targets. He took the chance that they would hit one and damage or sink the ship. Ike would make it happen and take the flack for it.

conservative was opposed to the FDR deficit spending and sit down strikes, but finally broke with FDR over the packing the supreme court which he felt concentrated too much power in the hands of the president. Imagine the difference had he been elected president in 1932 or 1940. Wallace, a social liberal was unpopular with Democrat leaders and was only on the ticket in 1940 at FDR's insistence. Wallace embraced FDR's vision far better than Garner. In 1944 the party leaders prevailed, Wallace was dumped and Truman, a total unknown was nominated. Somehow the party leaders got it right, they delayed the strong left turn of the party. Truman is one of the best presidents of the Twentieth Century. I will leave that though with this. He made two of the hardest decisions any American president has made, and he made both right. He approved the use of the Atom Bomb in spite of opposition from the scientists at Los Alamos and fired Douglas MacArthur, one of the most revered and over-rated American military men in our history and a man who felt he could be insubordinate to the president, his commander in chief. Regan hit a similar situation when he fired the Flight Controllers. These two presidents stand with Washington, Eisenhower and Lincoln as presidents who were willing to put their career on the line for what was right.

Roosevelt's government went oppressive on steroids when the Second World War started. He out-Wilson'ed Woodrow. The internment of the Americans of Japanese origin is a stain on our history and is well known. "The Supreme Court upheld the legality of the relocation order in Hirabayashi v. United States and Korematsu v. United States. Please remember this was "FDR's hand-picked court!" Early in 1945, Japanese-American citizens of "undisputed loyalty" were allowed to return to the West Coast, but not until March 1946 was the last camp closed."[55] Ironically March of 1946 was when the last of the German POW's were repatriated. Remember, by the time of the internment and the rulings in 1942 seven of the Supreme Court Justices were appointed by FDR. He had his court. Some of the impetus for this relocation was to protect the coast but there was pressure to remove the Japanese that can be tied to businessmen in California wanting to end the competition of Japanese businesses. I wonder how much negative impact taking these

---

[55] http://www.history.com/topics/world-war-ii/japanese-american-relocation

Americans out of the work force and making them dependent on the state harmed the war effort. It is well to note that many of the Americans of Japanese origins were not relocated from Hawaii, certainly a place with higher risk. But the Hawaiian businessmen were not as politically well-heeled and they also saw the Japanese descendants as valuable. This relocation is a serious stain on the American fabric and although it is often cited, the party affiliation of the perpetrators, Democrat is rarely mentioned.

What is little known of this period were the detention of Americans of Italian and German origin. "A total of 11,507 people of German ancestry were interned during the war. They comprised 36.1% of the total internments under the US Justice Department's Enemy Alien Control Program"[56] which did not include the Japanese. Although the number of Americans of Italian descent who were detained was much smaller, just over 3000, the abuses of power were much the same as the ones by Wilson in World War I. I find it interesting that those of German and Italian origin together compromise about 45% of the detainees, who are the other 55%? Like deaths, the number of political detainees is not important after the first one. After one, a million is just numbers.

The refusal of Roosevelt to allow blacks to be integrated into the military is certainly another travesty. His argument was this was not the time for a social experiment, but it was really cowing to and appeasing the southern Democrats. He needed them to keep the congress and having them support his election in 1944. His political future took second place to winning the war and social justice! Remember these Dixiecrats are the descendants of the slave owners and the writers of the Jim Crow laws, in fact some are the ones who helped write them and even some of them were officials in the KKK. An example is Robert Byrd, a KKK official and Democrat politician from West Virginia was in the House of Representatives from 1953-1959 and the US Senate from 1959 to 2010., an amazing 57 years of eating very well out of the taxpayer funded trough. Hillary Clinton called her mentor. Consider

---

[56] https://en.wikipedia.org/wiki/Internment_of_German_Americans Wikipedia cites Franca Iacovetta, Roberto Perin, and Angelo Principe, Enemies Within: Italian and Other Internees in Canada and Abroad, (University of Toronto Press, 2000), ISBN 0-8020-8235-1, p. 281

that! FDR was more interested in his dynasty than the good of the country in the war and after.

I am a pragmatist, where someone does well, I give them credit. Where they were allowed to fight on an equal basis of leadership, equipment and training, blacks served with honor. Sometimes they excelled in spite of the disadvantages. The Tuskegee Squadron, artillery units, and others served well. Tuskegee was the epitome of bomber escort. No squadron did it better. One artillery unit in Europe with an impressive record was overrun by German infantry during the Bulge and kept firing till the Germans were within their emplacements. Many of them died to the near point-blank German rifle fire, continuing to load and fire till killed, the ones taken captive were terribly treated. One unit of black cooks with about 100 men was caught in Bastogne and held a line as infantry, a task they were never trained to do. They were trained to bake bread and make eggs and stew, not in how to hold a line being attacked by a determined enemy. A few, literally a few paratroopers were seeded in the unit with them to provide support, and more important, advice and on the job training. To call this a less than optimal situation is a gross understatement. They and the paratroopers rose to the occasion, the paratroopers gave good advice, worked to help set up good defensive positions, told the cooks to not fire till they saw the whites of their eyes, the instructions of Jackson to his men at New Orleans in 1815. With the cooks' limited rifle training the paratroopers felt it was best if they engaged at close range where they would fire more effectively. They didn't want them to waste ammunition which was in short supply. At Bastogne, with the instruction of the paratroopers, the fire power of the M-1 and sheer determination these men followed the instructions and held what would have been called an impossible line. These men had good leadership and good weapons. They rose to the occasion. These cooks held their positions and killed Germans at close range with at least the efficiency they put into feeding troops. At some points attacking Germans had to climb over piles of dead German bodies only to be killed as they appeared. The line, "We fired our guns and the British came a coming, then there wasn't as many as there was a while ago" from the song, 'The Battle of New Orleans' fits if you replaced British with Germans. The paratroopers praised these men, all blacks. Like many white soldiers in the same war, they did what was needed. Bull Halsey said it well when one of his officers called him a great man. "There are no great men, only great situations that ordinary men rise to meet." Blacks in both wars showed that statement was not dependent on color. I want to mention here that the record of those who defended the Alamo lists one man only as 'Negro'. His name is unknown.

Allow me to make something clear. The super soldier theme that some want to attach to black soldiers is a myth, as is any indication they were inferior except in the lack of support they were given by the government. <u>There is no greater oppression than asking men to do a job that could cost them their lives and not giving them the best available leadership, tools and training to accomplish it.</u> I will comment that McAuffle, the commander at Bastogne had few resources but he gave that unit the best he could, good weapons, ammunition and the few paratroopers (I believe that number was 5) to guide them – note only because they did not have training. He gave what he had. They proved his confidence in them was not misplaced. The US Army short changed other blacks. After the battle, the paratroopers had nothing to say but good about those cooks. One of the paratroopers suggested they be transferred to the paratroopers. He knew they could fight. He had stood shoulder to shoulder with them and together they had won. There is no greater honor than to be said that you can be counted upon when the going gets tough, that another man would want you at his side or back when the going gets tough. There is a statement of trust, "You can have my back." It comes from a situation where two men are cut off, are surrounded and they sit back to back, one watching and defending 180 degrees, the other man's vulnerable area. In essence, those paratroopers, among the best fighting troops in the US Army saw something of value in these men. Sure, they lacked training, but they knew how to fight. They did not lack the will to do the job. They had demonstrated it.

Few are aware of it, but some civilian Americans were frozen in jobs during the war and their wages were also frozen at late 1941 levels. Prices increased considerably during

WASHINGTON, May 27 (AP) — A "freezing" of essential workers in critical war industries to their present jobs was decided upon to-day by the War Manpower Commission to stop "labor pirating," described as a severe interference with war production.

In this far-reaching move, the United States Employment Service was made the "sole hiring agency for critical skills in critical areas."

the war and these, mostly men in critical industrial positions, many in maintenance roles in the food and war industry, were harmed. I know about this first-hand because my dad was one of them. The company that he worked for, The Mann Corporation at the Aspers, PA food processing Plant, filed for draft exemption because he was the senior Maintenance person. [57] I will mention that only a few years before he started there, 'shoveling apples on the hill', the lowest level job in the plant. The food industry was considered as critical as arms manufacturing. You must continue to feed the troops and the home front to wage a war. He was exempted from the draft and would have been by age and dependents for some time, then when I was born without the exemption, but the exemption mandated that the corporation freeze his wages. I could understand the position freeze for the war effort, but the wage freeze harmed the family. The Mann corporation did not make any attempt to violate the wage freeze laws, but then, to do so would have cost them money and since my dad could not leave, had he done so he would have been picked up like a soldier who went AWOL, they have no reason to be concerned and offer a more money to insure he would stay. By 1945 our family would have been nearly destitute without my mom's working in the Masland Carpet plant in Carlisle where the carpet machinery was weaving and sewing canvas for tents, truck covers and tarps. My dad was in involuntary servitude, darned near slavery. The day the wage controls went off my dad got a significant pay raise, then in a few months a second significant one when they realized he was at risk to leave. A few years later the Mann Family sold the plant to Duffy Mott Company.[58] Initially my dad was asked to stay on 'to train others', but it was a "soft" relationship, he was not sure from one week to the next if he had a job. He started looking for a job, there were offers but nothing good showed up in the local area. He could move to New Jersey or Michigan for a good job, we

> The Commission also took further steps to make certain that men irreplaceable in war production may be deferred from the draft and remain at their work benches.

---

[57] Article from the Pottstown Mercury May 28, 1942

[58] Article Gettysburg Times September 13, 1950 I thought this happened earlier but I am not sure how long the court case was in progress. I do remember that my dad was sought by summons servers he evaded to testify on something at that time.

had an established home and were developing a truck farm and he did not want to leave.

A petition before the Middle District court at Scranton asking that the Adams Apple Corporation be declared bankrupt was dismissed today by Judge Frederick V. Folmer, sitting at Lewisburg. The dismissal followed a hearing at Harrisburg Monday.

The move cleared the way, attorneys said, for the completion of sale of the Adams Apple Products Corporation plant at Aspers to the Duffy-Mott Corporation of New York, one of the larger processing firms in the country.

Duffy-Mott has been in possession of the plant there for some time but transfer of the property was held up because of the bankruptcy proceeding instituted against

After a few months Motts made his position permanent, then later promoted him to Assistant Plant Manager. Even after that advancement he was still a consultant to and sometimes working with the maintenance crew when things went wrong. During their busy time, apple processing, he sometimes slept at the plant. But during the war he was vastly underpaid and that was never corrected. To give you an idea of the impact, the raises immediately after the price controls expired nearly tripled his pay and the Duffy Mott takeover added even more before the promotion, then added more with it.

I am sure that FDR manipulated the American people into World War II. He ran in 1940 on the platform, "He kept us out of war." It was implied he would continue that. His sales pitch was close to the one LBJ used in 1964, just before the Vietnam escalation. Wilson to some degree was guilty of being deceptive on war too. FDR did that, risking peril for the US because during that time we did not aggressively prepare for what was nearly inevitable. The US should have gone to a near war footing in late 1939 when Hitler took Europe. Even if the pace was slower than after Japan attacked Pearl, we had two years to build. Even in late 1941 when war was upon us FDR was convincing the people and the government that we would avoid war. He had to be careful to not be aggressive in building, least he damage the façade. We helped Britain and he indicated that was to keep us out. One of his phrases was aid to Britain with "everything short of war."

This editorial (below) by Bloak Carter appeared in the San Francisco Examiner May 17, 1940. It clearly defines the discussion of the FDR doctrine.

THE latest Gallup poll shows 66 per cent of the country supports a policy which refuses to send United States soldiers abroad, but which will give aid to the Allies on everything "short of war."

Analyze that. Is that a policy of wishful thinking? "Short of war" means aid in munitions, finances, credit and foodstuffs—everything "short of" actually going to war ourselves.

In theory it is fine. On paper it looks safe. Actually, what is it likely to produce?

Take the World War for a precedent. For two and a half years we supplied munitions, finances, credit and foodstuffs to the Allies, but we did not go to war. In a word, we were practicing then what 66 per cent of us think we should do now. We were aiding the Allies "short of war." What happened?

While Germany had the upper hand in the early stages, it didn't matter so much. When the Allied blockade pinch began to be felt, Germany began to grow desperate. Any man backed into a corner grows that way. He figures he has all to gain and nothing more to lose. He might as well adopt any tactics, below the belt included, as long as he can escape the corner and win.

Germany took reprisals against the United States. The grounds were that we were not neutral, in fact, we were acting as a storehouse for her enemies in Europe. She claimed that steps "short of war" were just as deadly against her as if we were actually in the war.

In other words, steps "short of war" eventually put us into war. Such steps, in the ultimate analysis, were literal acts of war. Yet 66 per cent of us vote the Gallup poll for the same thing over again. Mr. Roosevelt's foreign policy is based on "steps short of war."

Isn't this policy the equivalent to playing with matches and pretending we won't be burned?

Oh, we may THINK we can best the law of averages and render aid to the Allies with steps "short of war," but——

Reading the cables carrying such leaden news nowadays, I cannot help thinking of the name of Billy Mitchell. I cannot help thinking of the injustice done him by high ranking officers of the Army and Navy.

I cannot help thinking, without some anger, the way the Government, swivel chair aviators and brass hats, jeered at Billy Mitchell, blasted him as a "nut" for his persistent battle for a great air force for the Nation. I cannot help remembering how they rode him out of the Army because he dared to speak the truth.

At that time, we had some of our ships patrolling the Atlantic, but a war footing didn't happen till Pearl. The early battles of the war mostly went badly for us, we stopped and held the Japanese advance but at a terrible price in men and ships. The battles of Guadalcanal and those around Savo Island were fought on a shoestring. In "The Gallant Hours" Admiral Bull Halsey relates that in most of those battles, although we stopped the Japanese advance, had they pushed again shortly after we had nothing left to stop them. Thankfully, they were blooded enough that they did not press an attack although at times they had forces capable of brushing our surviving forces aside. One area there has so many sunken ships that it is called, 'Iron Bottom Sound.'

Another aspect of this was the military leadership that was still in "peacetime mode" at the end of 1941. FDR's de-emphasizing the military contributed to this. In this mode the men who keep their uniform straight, follow all the 'chicken shit rules' and write great reports excel and are promoted. In peacetime they captain ships and submarines and they lead regiments, companies and divisions. Some even become Admirals and Generals. Ones who tried to push for readiness were penalized, the most visible being Billy Mitchell who was courts marshalled for sinking a captured German battleship with aircraft when the admirals said air couldn't sink capital ships. Had his actions been taken as valid, not treated as insubordination, the sinking of the British Repulse and Prince of Wales and the attack Pearl might have been avoided. And Mitchel predicted in the early 1930's that the Japanese would someday attack American and start it on a Sunday morning with an attack on Pearl. But the strengths of those who rise in peacetime are in the minutia, not leading men in battle. When war comes, they are great as support and logistics people but not as battlefield and warship commanders. It took about a year after Pearl to weed out many of these. Many men died and battles were lost as this was being done. Organizational inertia is a deadly weapon in war.

No better example exists than the submarine arm, the unit that with about 30,000 men that went on to sink fifty one percent of the Japanese tonnage sunk by American forces. More than ten percent of them are still on patrol in the Pacific with the 63 submarines,[59] all commanded by

WASHINGTON, March 18.—(INS)—The Navy Department announced today the loss of two additional United States submarines, presumably the victims of Japanese counteraction in the far Pacific.

A communique identified the submarines as the Capelin, 1,525 tons, and the Sculpin, 1,475 tons.

Each submarine carried a crew of about seventy-five officers and men.

Among those lost, in addition to the commanders of both submarines, was Capt. John Philip Cromwell, divisional commander of submarines. Cromwell's home is at 1165 Harker Avenue, Palo Alto, Calif.

Commander John Cromwell, the highest-ranking officer in this force. I want to show the caliber of the men who sailed these steel cigars. Cromwell was aboard the Sculpin[60] as a wolf pack commander, one of the times we used this tactic. The only reason for a divisional commander to be

---

[59] Submarines are not listed by the service as 'sunk', they are 'still on patrol.'

[60] The Sculpin was the sister ship of the Squalus which sunk in training May 23, 1939. Twenty nine of the crew died, thirty three were rescued. The Squalus was salvaged, repaired and renamed the Sailfish. After the Sculpin sinking, some of its crew were rescued and placed on the carrier Chūyō, the Sailfish torpedoed it and they were lost.

on a submarine was to lead a wolf pack. Note that each sub had a commander who was lost.

Yes, we blasted the German Wolf Packs, a propaganda theme, but we used them. Cromwell was on board a submarine when it was damaged by depth charges and forced to the surface. The men got off and the quartermaster was ready to open the ballast tank vents to scuttle the boat.[61] Cromwell was sitting at the chart table. The sailor told him he needed to leave, the other crewmembers were off, (some of them survived) they were scuttling, sinking the sub on purpose to prevent capture. Cromwell told him to go on, he knew things about the future plans that the Japanese would want to know, they would cost American lives if he revealed them, he was not leaving. Cromwell went down with the boat. Such was the men who sailed these. But in the early months of the war these boats[62] were commanded by people who were not wartime commanders. They wore the straightest uniforms and wrote the best reports. Worse, their most lethal weapon, the torpedo had a serious flaw.

In 1942 the submarines had torpedoes that hit ships and did not explode because of a faulty firing pin. This is a piece of steel that sticks out in front of the torpedo. For some reason, this critical steel pin had not been hardened. It hit the ship, flattened, did not hit the primer behind it and did not fire the warhead. The failure to explode was known but the cause was not. And the organization inertia from peacetime delayed finding this for months – they did not want to waste one torpedo in a test firing! Within hours of a test fire of a torpedo with sand in the warhead, the cause and a field fix was known, the pins were removed and hardened by heating each pin red hot with an acetylene

---

[61] Ballast tanks on subs are large tanks that if filled with water to make the boat heavy enough to sink. Fill them with air, the boat floats. When under the sea, 'blowing the tanks' means forcing compressed air into them which pushes the water out. The tanks have two valves one on the top and one on the bottom. To 'blow the tanks' and surface the top valves are closed to keep the air in and the bottom ones opened to let the water be forced out. To dive the bottom are open to let water in and the top opened to let the air out. The sub had 'blown the tanks' with the bottom open and the top closed. To send her to the bottom all that was needed was to open the top vents.

[62] Submarines are boats, not ships.

torch and quenching it in a bucket of sea water to harden the steel! But men risked themselves and their boats to get into a firing position to see the torpedo bounce off the target rather than blowing a hole in its side! I shudder when I think that a sub with effective torpedoes may have sunk a ship with troops or ammunition that survived to help hold islands and kill American soldiers. When a weapon fails, it may have impact outside the immediate action. The magnetic exploders that were also being used had a flaw, they were designed in the US, but no allowance was made to accommodate the difference in the earth's magnetic field in the south Pacific. That caused many of the torpedoes to not explode. The magnetic exploder allowed the fish to run under the ship and explode, creating terrible damage by the upward vented explosion. When it worked even sizeable ships had such damage that one torpedo sent them to the bottom. This too took months to fix.

The 'report writing commanders' were being relieved when it became evident that they could not command a warship. Again, inertia was in place. When it was evident that a submarine commander was not a warrior, he was replaced after two lackluster patrols, often by his executive officer. If the exec came back with one lackluster patrol, he was also replaced. These men, about half of the submarine captains, were moved to other positions they were well suited for, several commanded hospital ships, many served well in desk jobs, some support ships, important positions but they were just not suited to command a submarine. Mentally they could not fight a boat. Similar activities happened in other services. Remember that when you are in a submarine, tracking a target, you are very vulnerable. The stakes are lives, including your own. Some men just can't do that. They are not bad men, only that they lack the skill.

Gregory (Pappy) Boyington was a peacetime military misfit, didn't know or didn't care about the starched uniform or rules but he served with distinction as a fighter pilot in China before the war, then as a leader of the Black Sheep Squadron until he was shot down. (Press and Sun-Bulletin Binghamton NY August 29, 1945)

Starched uniforms didn't matter to him. Many of his unit including him had bad conduct records. To Pappy, creases in the uniform didn't matter, off duty brawls were not important, removing Japanese from the fight with any means available was all that mattered. But let's remember that he saw first-hand in China what the Japanese military was doing to civilians. He joined Bob Johnson as one of the high scoring aces in World War II. Both broke Eddie Rickenbacher's World War I record of planes shot down, Johnson on his last flight before rotation, Boyington just seconds before he was shot down and wound up in a Japanese POW camp. Books "Thunderbolt" and "Baa Baa Black Sheep" detail their war time service. Boyington and Johnson did not have the highest scores of WW2 but Johnson was rotated to the states after breaking the record and was not returned to combat. He did bond tours. Boyington was shot down before most of the experienced pilots of the Japanese Air arm were taken out. These two fought in a different war than the ones who were in the last days of the war when most of the enemy were relatively inexperienced. Also in the pacific, the F4U was just coming into service as was the Wildcat.

But then, to understand rules and their sometimes lack of value, Johnson scored a 4.7 percent on his aerial gunnery and was signed off to go overseas. Five percent is passing! Imagine this. The highest scoring ace in the European Theatre failed air-to-air gunnery! There were at least twenty-eight[63] German fighter pilots who may have contested that ruling had they lived to tell about it after he got on their tail. Go figure.

Douglas Badder a British fighter pilot lost both legs before the war in a crash he had while violating RAF rules. He returned to duty during the Battle of Britain. He was a high scoring ace, was shot down, a POW and tried to escape. Like Boyington his record was somewhat tarnished. A phenomenal book, "Reach for the Sky" is his biography.

There is an adage that it is not the size of the dog in the fight but the size of the fight in the dog that matters. Johnson proved that it was not the gunnery score but the ability to see enemy, see the advantage, know his and his opponent's aircraft, see how to get on another plane's tail and stay there till the bullets took effect. In a dog fight the misses do not matter, only the hits. That was more important than the artificial measurement, the score. I wonder how many American airmen's lives were saved by the officer who bent the rules and signed off for Johnson to go to Europe. A German fighter pilot taken out of the mix today is not back tomorrow to kill. But the military clung to some of its peacetime habits including segregation.

Although FDR was not directly responsible for some of this, the leadership from the top sets the tone. The Mitchel courts marshal set a bad tone. The castigation of George Patton and removing him from leadership for a time pulled one of the three most effective battlefield commanders of the war out of a field position for nothing but Public Relations when he was desperately needed. That decision had to be at least given a nod by George Marshall and FDR. In one of my novels I credit George Patton with saying "Brad (Omar Bradley) is the third best General in the US Army." This is substantiated by various statements he made. I know George considered General "Vinegar Joe" Stillwell second. Of course, George knew who was best. George S. Patton. I happen to agree with him. Jackson of 1812 and Sherman 1864-5 must

---

[63] Johnson was credited with a kill on one of his probables based on a later confirmation. These were frequent, Boyington had one he shot down just before his crash but was not reported until he was released. Others were credited because of German records or released POW reports. The US rules on confirmation were the strictest.

be the hands down contenders for four and five. Some will ask, "Where is Ike?" I respect him, but General Dwight David Eisenhower was never proven to be a great field general, however he uniquely filled a role in World War II that I am sure was critical and I know of no other man living at the time who could have filled it. In that role, he was not only the best, I know of no contender. Douglass MacArthur tried to be both Ike and Patton in the Pacific and had the credentials for neither. He was not worthy of shining their boots. Ike's big accomplishments were keeping Brad and George from killing the British Bernard Montgomery and keeping Monty from mucking up the war effort more than he did without splitting the Atlantic Alliance. In my opinion the invasion and occupation of Europe was impeded more and more lives were lost by Monty's actions than by those of any two German officers. It would have been a lot worse without Ike.

I want to mention Vinegar Joe Stilwell here, one of the least known and very important figures in the War. He was in charge of the China Burma Theatre and I am not sure any other man, including Patton or Bradley would have done it as well. It is why I rate Joe at high as I do. Where George and Brad never got the supplies and men they wanted, Joe never got half of what he needed but he made do with what he had and drove the Japanese crazy with effective use of men and material. He was the oldest American General and was in the jungle with his men, directing the battles. He was on the end of a precarious supply line that was incapable of giving him what he really needed even when it was functioning at full capacity, which it rarely was. I find it ludicrous when the Government claimed that in Vietnam the Viet Cong was using tactics they did not understand. Stillwell was the original leader of a jungle insurgency! Maybe someone should have studied his campaigns like they have the ones of Lee and Meade at Gettysburg, neither of which were stellar performances.

If you have ever seen films of men in shorts, cranking a generator to run a radio, that is probably a film of Stilwell's men. The oldest General in the war was out there in that jungle with them. I will give you an idea of what that was like. A man can produce for a short time 1/6 of a horsepower, 120 watts. When receiving that radio burned more than a quarter of that and a battery stored the excess. When transmitting it burned nearly three times that, depleting the battery. The guy turning the crank was going full out to keep it on the air and in jungle heat. It is only a representation of what they did and Stilwell was there with them, not in an office. The American Army has produced some fantastic leaders and soldiers. Vinegar Joe should be one of those who is so honored. I can understand him and his men not being featured while they were there, his having one more mouth to feed (a reporter) would not have been wise, neither would have letting the Japanese know any more than what they could define. But he should have been after the war.

Unfortunately, FDR and those in DC made it more difficult for these men, sometimes impeding them more than the Germans and Japanese.

The UN

Face it, the UN is a government, an ineffective one of course, but a government. Many point to its 'successes' which include the naming of Israel as a nation in 1948. Although I see that as a right decision the declaration was so flawed that it really looked to any astute observer to be the design for the extinction of the Jews in the nation. If you wish to study this subject in detail there is a book, 'O Jerusalem'[64] by Larry Collins and Dominique Lapierre that is a well-researched history of this period. Let us face it, the British were complicit with the UN in setting up the Jews for slaughter at the hands of the descendants of the Moors who were defeated by Charles Martel at Tours. It also set the stage for the current problems in Palestine.

I would like to mention here that there is so much commentary on the problems between Jews and Arabs as the roadblock to peace in the Middle East. I point to one thing. These two forces have not met on the field of battle for nearly 40 years while one Arab nation has attacked another. Maybe we are working on resolving the wrong problem.

The UN oppression varies between oppression by action or by inaction. If you read the high-sounding descriptions the UN is to be a force for

---

[64] Available on Kindle Store for $4.00 - a steal. It was originally published in 1972 and re-published in 2006. It is one of those books that is a 'must read' to understand history.

peace, justice and freedom. For the Muslims and the communists, peace is defined as Muslim or communist domination and freedom as doing what the leaders say. The UN is a classic example of the inmates running the asylum. The biggest offenders in human rights get to preside over UN actions on human rights. The criminals are enforcing the laws! From the UN web page, the Commission is defined.

> The United Nations Commission on Human Rights was established in 1946 to weave the international legal fabric that protects our fundamental rights and freedoms. Composed of 53 States members, its brief expanded over time to allow it to respond to the whole range of human rights problems and it set standards to govern the conduct of States. It also acted as a forum where countries large and small, non-governmental groups and human rights defenders from around the world voiced their concerns.

Freedom and rights? Let's look at the composition from the site.[65] African States 15, Asian States 12, Eastern European States 5, Latin American & Caribbean States 11, Western Europe & Other States 10. The author will note that it was difficult to find the names of the countries! When something is hidden, something is wrong.

This was replaced by the United Nations Human Rights Council. When viewed realistically this was nothing more or less than a name change to confuse. The charter, again from the UN page is:

> The Human Rights Council is an inter-governmental body within the United Nations system made up of 47 States responsible for the promotion and protection of all human rights around the globe.

I look at who is on that council. Note the ones that are not underlined.

Afghanistan, Angola, <u>Australia</u>, <u>Belgium</u>, Brazil, Burundi, Chile, China, Côte d'Ivoire, Croatia, Cuba, Democratic Republic of the Congo, Ecuador, Egypt, Ethiopia, Georgia, <u>Germany</u>, Hungary, Iraq, <u>Japan</u>, Kenya, Kyrgyzstan, Mexico, Mongolia, Nepal, Nigeria, Pakistan, Panama,

---

[65] Composition of the UN Commission on Human rights
http://www.ohchr.org/EN/HRBodies/CHR/Pages/Membership.aspx

Peru, Philippines, Qatar, Republic of Korea, Rwanda, Saudi Arabia, Senegal, Slovakia, Slovenia, South Africa, Spain, <u>Switzerland,</u> Togo, Tunisia, Ukraine, United Arab Emirates, <u>United Kingdom of Great Britain and Northern Ireland</u>, <u>United States of America</u>, Venezuela (Bolivarian Republic of)

I will bluntly say there is no country on that list that does not have blemishes in both its past and present. None of them are blameless including the US. Let us face it, governments are created and operated by people and even the best of them fail at times. Other than the ones underlined I question them being on the list. There are a couple more including the Philippines and Brazil that have blemishes on their records but are working hard, improving and should have a right to sit there. South Africa, for long a country noted for abuse of rights of blacks is now becoming an anti-white racist country with terrible abuses of whites, matching or exceeding the abuses of blacks. Two wrongs don't make a right and whites are now in fear for their lives.

But let us look at the ones that have current issues that are serious. Afghanistan, Pakistan, Iraq, Syria, and Saudi Arabia leap off the page as ones that allow significant discrimination of women and religion. Cuba is far from a model human rights leader. Angola severely limits freedoms of assembly, association, speech, and press. Burundi has seen an increase in politically motivated killings. Chile allows discrimination against indigenous populations; societal violence and discrimination against women, and children. Côte d'Ivoire seems to be in turmoil and rights are not being protected. Democratic Republic of the Congo has serious violations, such as arbitrary executions, rape, torture and cruel, inhuman and degrading treatment are pervasive, committed mostly by the army, police and intelligence services. Egypt has effectively banned protests and freedom of expression, and it has imprisoned its opponents. Women and members of religious minorities are subject to discrimination. Ethiopia has a list of violations that are appalling. Georgia has issues with accountability of law enforcement. And the list goes on.

I wasn't half-way through, got frustrated and quit looking at the countries at this point. This organization is not a travesty. It is a farce.

One comment here, discrimination against Christians is <u>never</u> cited except as obliquely in Egypt where they are called religious minorities which are Christians and Jews. In the US we still have a way to go but for the most part human rights violations are against the law, not the law of the land. In most cases (should be all) they are aggressively prosecuted. We haven't arrived. We must always press to be better. America should strive to be the best in this area. If every nation would do that, human rights violations would become a rarity, an illegal act, not a government policy. The US is charged with the mistreatment of gays, homosexuals and transgenders. Fine. In the US it is against the law and those who offend are at risk of prosecution. The argument is that we do not consider them to have special status and rights above others. But in some Muslim countries killing these would be legal. Somehow, I see a significant difference, but the UN Commission doesn't, in fact while castigating the US, they ignore the others.

The UN has a document, Agenda 21. It is the blueprint for oppression under the high-sounding liberal word, "Sustainability." It details what is needed to attain this. It includes no personal ownership or property, vehicles, or weapons. If you want to build something, you ask for permission and rent the land from the government. If you want a vehicle, you ask for permission and rent it from the government. If you want a weapon, you ask for permission and rent it from the government. The government plans, allocates use, controls. The government decides what parcel of land, what vehicle, what weapon you get and even if you get one! If the government bureaucrat doesn't think you need it, it doesn't fit the government plan or don't need the one that serves your need, too bad. Read that and think about the Soviet Union under Communism. It is that path to that. The UN and the globalists in the US who have signed on to it are paving the way. At one time state governors and members of the House and Senate were signing on.

Look at the long range on this. Every totalitarian society has confiscated weapons to consolidate power. This includes ones from Nazi Germany to Communism. In the US it has been done by controlling licenses and making ownership illegal. Some cities have done that and the South after reconstruction made it illegal for blacks to have the ability to defend themselves. Oppression rears its evil head in many places. Add to that the ability to control free movement by controlling access to vehicles. If there is anything that is basic to the US, it is the ability to travel freely. However, if the government can limit individual vehicle access, they can push us to mass transit, use an ID card system, microchips, facial recognition and they can control our travel or at least track it. The technology to do it is already in place in Communist China. It is all about taking freedoms in the name of something that is not a proven problem. Add to this the aspect of self-driving cars which must be accurately tracked, and services like Uber which are ordered over the internet using a credit card. They may not know if you traveled in the car, but they will know who procured it. And do you really think the self-driving car will not have a camera, possibly video of you making the trip? The car will have to be on the 4G network or some equivalent and connected to servers that are on the internet. With the maintenance of Windows, Linux, Unix, MACs, tablets and cell phones being done from the internet, all are connected. My Raspberry pi linux servers are behind a router that is solid and is NAT'ting the IP addresses. Is my network secure? As long as nobody really wants in, yes. A determined hack is going to get through. Honestly, I can't be sure the FBI hasn't hacked me. I have considered asking for my FBI file. But will I get it? Will it be redacted?

I would like to address the idea of sustainability. In the 1950's if you believed the so-called experts we were running out of oil. Our world-wide reserves would be gone in 10, 20 years depending on which doomsday soothsayer you listened to. This article in the Kilgore News Herald in Texas shows the oil industry refuting it. To help make their predictions come true the left put more and more restrictions on drilling in the US till it essentially stopped and we were dependent on Arab oil.

The industry can tell the public, for instance, that the yearly additions to our proved reserves in the last 10 years have totalled 23 billion barrels.

This is more than all the oil produced in the nation during the first 80 years of the industry's life. Our reserves have continued to grow in spite of repeated predictions that we are running out of oil.

The crisis of 1973-4 showed us how dependent we were and we did NOTHING to change that. There was no real oil shortage, the Arabs just closed the tap.

In the 1980s the places to put garbage were nearly gone. We would have no place to put trash in ten years.

We had a shortage of natural gas that caused laws restricting connections and thermostat settings.

In the 1950s an ice age was predicted for some time after 2000. Now the same group of scientists are predicting melting ice caps and global warming. We just had a March that had fantastic amounts of snow. With the liberal North East being buried under snow and the liberal Southern California being burned and buried under mud, I have a better explanation than man made global warming. Maybe God is pissed off with American Liberals. They seem to be getting the bad weather.

Today the US, whose oil reserves were considered almost depleted in 1950 is an exporter of oil, the price had hit a very low and has rebounded to a level more representative of the cost of production. The low was an artificial low created by dumping by the Arabs to shut down American and Canadian production because it was a little more expensive. It was "cutting the competition off at the knees" by the Arabs selling below cost, an illegal practice in most countries and on the world market. Pennsylvania and neighboring states are producing enough natural gas that the big problem is transporting it, which is also a problem for the oil production. Ironically the same groups who predicted disaster are

The National Transportation Safety Board sent a team of investigators to the site. The board had begun a major investigation of a late December crude rail accident in Casselton, N.D., which led to the evacuation of more than 1,000 residents.

Crude shipments by rail have shot up twenty-fivefold in the last several years as producers rush oil from newly developing shale fields to refineries along routes that are not served by pipelines. McCown said he believed the nation needed not only better tank cars and safer train operations, but also more pipelines.

fighting the construction of pipelines. I am not sure that they are not doing that to help their predictions of shortages look good. Delaying those pipelines is causing more crude to be shipped by rail, a less safe method of transport. Although much more products move over pipelines, the deaths caused by accidents is much lower than rail. But then, we are far more concerned about the deaths of spotted owls and bats than people. Article from the LA Times May 1, 2014.

Landfills are a concern, but technology, private investment, and recycling has taken the edge off that issue. Today over 99% of the content of lead acid batteries, car batteries, is being recovered and reused. This was initiated by a private business that saw the recoverable value in the lead, sulfuric acid, and even the plastic cases and started collection and recovery operations. The company that is processing them is still looking for ways to increase the recovery percent. Every pound they recover is something they can sell. What they cannot recover they have to pay to haul away as trash. We are doing a lot with plastics and paper and only need to do more.

Pennsylvania has a recycling law that has some flaws but is essentially a good one. I live alone and have little garbage and trash. My recyclables volume is rarely less than the trash volume! Add to that my bush and tree trimmings that once went to a land fill and now several trailer loads go to Spring Valley Mulch where they are chopped up by a private firm that sells the mulch. As an aside, if I take the same limbs to the county facility, I pay to dump them to be mulched. If I take them to Spring Valley which is about 2 miles closer, I dump free. They like my tree limbs. Guess where my tree limbs go? They are mulched and Spring Valley is a significant supplier of mulch in the area. Since they have been in business for some time and seem to be financially stable, they must be making some money doing that. Recycling to use the word loosely can be financially and environmentally beneficial. I would love to see steel, copper, glass and aluminum recycling, possibly a bin at the local fire company or municipal building. It appears that only if government gets involved does it go sour.

Waste Management company headed by Scott Wagner has been running a clean landfill and trash hauling firm for years. As an astute businessman he is looking to make a profit and be sustainable. If he runs out of landfill space, he is out of business. The only government item in the mix here is the County incinerator – an electric co-gen facility and very little of our garbage goes there. It is a good operation however many of these government-owned facilities are tax money pits. The one in Harrisburg nearly bankrupted the city, with the help of an incompetent mayor. With her replacement the city is pulling out of the mess. Get the government involved in something and I can guarantee it will not be profitable. The city parking lots were handed over to a private firm that is paying rent rather than the city running them as a burden to the taxpayer. Is there a theme here?

The UN Agenda 21 is a vehicle to bring about a One World Government and it will be a non-benevolent one. Worse, some US senators and representatives in the US have signed on to the concept.

President George H. W. Bush was one of the 178 heads of government who signed the final text of the agreement at the Earth Summit in 1992, and in the same year Representatives Nancy Pelosi, Eliot Engel and William Broomfield spoke in support of United States House of Representatives Concurrent Resolution 353, supporting implementation of Agenda 21 in the United States.[66] All who have are globalists or socialists, but then there is little difference.

I might add that there are other addle headed members of our government who support it.

LBJ

The LBJ platform of 1964 is very well summed up in this paragraph from Wikipedia.

> While Johnson campaigned on a platform of limited involvement in Vietnam and continuation of funding for social programs, Goldwater called for substantial cuts in social programs, suggesting that Social Security become optional, and suggested the use of nuclear weapons in Vietnam if necessary. Goldwater believed that the Tennessee Valley Authority should be sold into the private sector. On foreign policy, Goldwater's beliefs differed sharply from those of his opponent, who advocated limited involvement in Vietnam, maintaining that he would not send "American boys nine or ten thousand miles

---

[66] https://en.wikipedia.org/wiki/Agenda_21

from home to do what Asian boys ought to be doing for themselves." Goldwater, however, accused Johnson and the Democratic party of having given in on the issue of Communist aggression.[67]

Goldwater was proven wrong on one point. Johnson had not given in on the issue of Communist aggression. We must remember he was a politician and an egomaniac. There was no way he wanted to be the president that succeeded JFK and could not get elected on his own. He had to play to the anti-war sentiment in his own party. He had to win. Twenty years before he won an election in Texas by ballot box stuffing that was so obvious, even to the party faithful that he was called Landslide Johnson. The night of the election he

> And next, but not least: It was Abe who fixed the opposition after Lyndon's election to the Senate in 1948 when the opposition sought court relief on the grounds the way the election was conducted smelled like 100 acres of dead skunks.
> It was in that election LBJ won also the title "Landslide Lyndon." First results showed he had lost the election, then 200 votes "turned up" resulting in LBJ's "landslide of less than 100 votes. Some of those "turned up" votes came from the cemetery, some who saw the voter list claimed.

---

[67] https://en.wikipedia.org/wiki/Barry_Goldwater_presidential_campaign,_1964

Anyway, the Supreme Court had been asked to have a look at the Texas election, but Abe Fortas fixed it so the court kept its hands off. (Just for double protection, the ballot box dissappeared, but we don't imagine Abe had to go to Texas to arrange that).

The point of all this is to suggest that Fortas is something more than crony ordinaire to Lyndon Johnson. He's been fixer, and if anybody has been ahead of him in the fixers — was trailing by 100 votes. Two hundred ballots were found in a box in a car trunk to hand the win to him. Every ballot in the box was for him. Article from the Odessa American, July 26, 1968. Note how carefully It was fixed? The end justified the means.

LBJ had an election to win in 64 and in true Johnson fashion cared little about the truth if that had to be sacrificed to win. In his mind the truth could easily be sacrificed to win, a Hitlerian concept. Like Nixon a few years later, winning became everything. As far as we know, Johnson just didn't break the law in 1964, he just lied. It is fortunate for many in DC lying and stupidity are not crimes. Remember the line by WJC, "I did not have sex with that woman, Monica Lewinski." It was not only a lie, it was stupid. There was too much evidence to the contrary without the semen stained blue dress.

Johnson had little understanding of the military. He was an officer in the Army Reserve but had seen only one "action" in World War II before being returned to the states after a short time in a combat zone. He was returned from the South Pacific on an FDR order that no elected officials could be in the war zone. In that 'action' for which he got a

Lyndon is now telling congressional colleagues this story on himself. He was stationed temporarily in New Guinea, and had just participated in a bombing raid over Jap territory. After the raid, Johnson got out his motion picture camera and was about to take some pictures of American troops. But he had trouble, and sat for some time in a straw-thatched hut trying to fix the camera.

commendation, he was flying as an observer on a recon mission in a B-17 that saw no fighters or flack, had no mechanical situations and landed normally. No other member of the crew got any commendation. It looked good on a "politician war hero's" military record. Note the embellished story in the Tampa Times November 10, 1942. Go figure. John McCain is not my favorite, but he was a pilot, was in the fight. I am not sure his military record was impressive, but he did fly where bullets were fired at him. LBJ did not.

LBJ saw social programs as the way to keep people on the neo-plantation and voting for him. I believe in 1964 he was looking at a nearly ten-year presidency, just under two years of JFK's term and two of his own. There was no indication, to the contrary until he announced he would not run in 68, even as late as this March 25, 1968 Orlando Star article it appeared likely. I believe he was a leader in seeing this in the keeping the Democrat electorate both loyal and expanding. To

RECENTLY JOHNSON has called for O'Brien's political advice or aid only occasionally. There have been reports that O'Brien would be tapped to run LBJ's election campaign after the convention, but he could be tapped for the vice presidential nomination instead to pacify the Kennedys and McCarthy.

maintain his political financial base, he had to have military spending at a significant level. Terms like 'guns and butter' came out. The federal government had gobs of money. We could afford both. The 'Great Society' strengthened one pillar of the arch, military spending was the other. But even as Michael Moore recognized in "Canadian Bacon' it is hard to increase or even maintain military spending unless there is an enemy and North Vietnam looked better than Canada. I am not sure that Moore was not one of Johnson's advisors. The Gulf of Tonkin incident was the vehicle to make it happen.

Look at programs from the era like the FB-111, a program that was rife with waste mainly because of political dickering and interference. A government project has never built a decent plane. Private industry, men like the Wright Brothers, Boeing, and Kelly Johnson have. The U-2, the SR-71, F-117, the F4-U, the B-17 all were built in spite of government interference. The B-17 actually violated the Army requirements for a two engine bomber - but when its capability was demonstrated it was adopted. Developing it nearly broke Boeing. The Langley Aerodrome is a government funded and built plane at Smithsonian. It never was successful. A lot of money was spent with very little progress. The Wrights, spending their own money could not be wasteful. They worked out as many problems before an attempted flight. One of the things they developed was the wind tunnel, a way to do some testing with small models. Langley had government funds to replace a crashed aircraft. Another crash? No problem. Build another plane. We saw some of that in the space program. It was a government attitude problem, not a technical one. Langley, like Curtis did not recognize the big problem of flight was control and he never got it. Curtis finally got that figured out when later he merged with the Wrights. Curtis and Wright separately had developed various aspects of flight. Together they were great. Langley never did get it.

At this point LBJ planned to run again in 1968. Unlike Truman who succeeded FDR less than a year after his death and was unable to run for the third term, Kennedy's death November 22, 1963 was late enough in the term with only a year and a couple months left, for him to run again. A win in 1964 and then in 1968 would have made him easily the longest serving president other than FDR who was not impacted by the Twenty Second Amendment. An LBJ win in 1968 would go down in history. I believe he pulled out of the race in 1968 because he knew he could not win. Imagine the chagrin had he lost to the man who JFK beat, albeit the JFK win was with help from the Daley ballot box stuffing in Cook County. But then, LBJ knew how to make that happen too.

If you look at what the loss to Kennedy in the 1960 primary did to LBJ emotionally, you would understand, this guy could not handle loss. He had one very large ego and a terrible inferiority complex. He got into politics with his wife's daddy's money. He came out of the 1960 race badly wounded. People close to the then vice-president in mid-1963, just before the assassination of JFK noted that Johnson was drinking heavily and there was concern about him committing suicide. His ego was bruised by being put in second place on the 1960 ticket. He had gone from the leader of the Senate to the Vice President and with Robert F. Kennedy driving things in the White House, a fall from one of the most important men in DC to a position not far above the White

House janitor in the JFK regime. They had run a brutal primary fight. Even after the campaign and election, the hatchet was still out. And there were other inputs. Lady Bird Johnson loathed Jackie for stealing the first lady position from her and it was out in the open and well known. I am sure she fed high octane fuel to the fire. It was her daddy's money that had been used to kick start LBJ's political career. But for her gender she would be in the limelight. Actually, she had more of the demeanor for it than LBJ. Honestly, I knew of the animosity at the time and wondered if LBJ had some hand in the assassination or even more likely, Lady Bird. My dad, an astute observer said the same thing. She had the connections in Texas, even more than LBJ. Her connections in Texas were generational, his political. But for the accident of gender, Lady Bird would have had daddy's money to fuel a political career but in 1940's Texas, a woman could never have won election. It was up to Lady Bird to pick a male companion and push him. I have read Shakespeare's Macbeth and have seen the fictional Macbeth's wife and Lady Bird in the same light.

Today I am sure JFK's death was at the collective hands of Lee Harvey Oswald and John K. Hinky. I for one do not believe the one shooter theory of the Arlan Specter and the Warren Commission and never did from the time I read it less than a year after it was released. It has as many holes as a sponge. It has self-contradictions. Specter was a political hack who had an agenda, please LBJ – who wanted the matter ended quickly without impacting his election run. It should have been called the Specter Commission because he ran the show. Earl Warren was there to make it look respectable, something Arlan could never have done.

Kennedy had a minor wound from a fragment of Oswald's first bullet and may have survived Oswald's second shot that hit him in the throat. The throat wound was a possibly but not certainly fatal. Lee Harvey Oswald only fired 2 shots. The CIA and mob theories are interesting pieces of conjecture. The AR-15 round, the one fired accidentally by John Hinkey, a member of the secret service was instantly deadly.[68] It

---

[68] Check the book "Mortal Error, the Death of JFK". It is the only explanation of the shooting that makes any sense, the work of a ballistics expert with impeccable credentials. It does not need the convoluted and distorted "grassy

blew out a portion of his brain and the direction of travel was wrong for a shot from the building but correct for from near street level. Both wounds were inconsistent with a shot from the grassy knoll, the conspiracy theorist holy grail. A bullet from the weapon Oswald was using would almost certainly have created a deadly head wound but not one like that. A bullet from the grassy knoll would have blown out the back, not the front of his head. The view of the Zaphruder film does not accurately show the damage. But the Secret Service and most likely RFK conspired that day to cover the accidental shooting. Arlan Specter and some others on the Warren Commission bowed to LBJ and pushed for an early decision, to have it out well before the 1964 election. Looking at Specter's involvement in the Warren Commission I am very sure he knew the truth because he rejected any input that would have pointed away from his theory. Witnesses who would have contradicted his scenario were not called, were called and sent home without testifying and there was not one ballistics expert on either the investigation team or the list of witnesses. The most damning evidence was the Secret Service officers who swore under oath they had no weapons on site other than .38 revolvers and the Warren report has a picture of Hinky with the rifle. Actually, there is another published picture of him with it at Parkland Hospital. The AR-15, a long gun, cannot be confused with a .38, a stub nosed revolver. No person, even one not familiar with firearms could make that mistake. The Warren Report is a fantastic fictional work, mostly the literary work of Arlan.

To see LBJ's duplicity, we go to this day in history, July 28, 1965, less than nine months after the election.

---

knoll" pictures or Arlan Specter's magic bullet. It is just an accidental discharge of a weapon that is on at least two pictures in the *Warren Report*, both showing it in Hinkey's hands, a weapon the Secret Service swore under oath was not there! Hinky was not an agent and should never have been in the chase car and should never have had the weapon. Someone should have gone to jail for perjury. Until I read that book, I had this nagging thought that one of the Johnsons, probably Lady Bird, not Lyndon engineered JFK's death. A second ballistics expert was commissioned to study it to make a movie about how it was flawed. His study convinced him the book was accurate, he was able to contribute additional evidence that was misses and the movie was made. I have seen both the book and movie; they are credible and scholarly works.

President Lyndon B. Johnson announces that he has ordered an increase in U.S. military forces in Vietnam, from the present 75,000 to 125,000. Johnson also said that he would order additional increases if necessary. He pointed out that to fill the increase in military manpower needs, the monthly draft calls would be raised from 17,000 to 35,000.[69]

Johnson impressed an additional 18,000 men into military service EVERY MONTH to make up the jungle warfare fodder. In all 58,220 men died in that war.[70] I will add that 36,756, well over half of them died under LBJ. The highest death toll per year of 16,899 occurred in 1968 and 1967 was 11,373, Johnson's last two years in office. The 16,899 is 325 deaths a week, 46 a day! LBJ and McNamara were feeding men into the battle at a metered rate, men were dying, and we were not achieving victory. Nixon's first year in office, 1969 had 11,780, only slightly above LBJ's second highest year.[71] Nixon was clearly winding down the war. Say what you will about Nixon, in 1969 5,119 less American soldiers died than in 1968, that is 98 each week, down from the over 300 a week under Johnson. I don't consider this impressive, just tracking in the right direction. I believe Nixon was looking for a way to disengage and applaud his efforts but during that year more than 200 men died each week.

As an aside, in addition to the names of 58,212 men there are the names of 8 women on the Vietnam wall. I know only one name, Pamela J. Donavan, a nurse. I have not looked for another because she represents all eight of them to me. She died in theatre of a viral infection by a rare virus. I only know her name by coincidence. When I visited the wall, I took three close-up pictures each having about 50 names and when I was looking at them later, I saw her name near the bottom of the picture and researched her. She was an Irish immigrant who wanted to serve. She gave her life in Vietnam. She was there

---

[69] http://www.history.com/this-day-in-history/johnson-announces-more-troops-to-vietnam
[70] https://www.archives.gov/research/military/vietnam-war/casualty-statistics.html
[71] https://www.archives.gov/research/military/vietnam-war/casualty-statistics.html

working to save lives of the wounded. I salute Pamela Donavan and the other seven along with the 59,212 men, RIP.

The oppression of conscription was made even worse by its not being uniformly applied. Blacks were conscripted at higher rates than whites, poor whites more than rich ones, and many went to Vietnam and died. At one point in the war black casualties were running nearly 25 percent of total when they were 14 percent of the in-theatre troops and 10.6 percent of the population. They were over-represented in both deployed (1.4 times whites) and deaths (2.5 times whites). Some of this was the reflection of them being higher numbers of the most recent conscripts, ground combat troops and the lowest level troops who were exposed to the heat of battle. I question if maybe some of these were sent there with less than adequate training. As I have said elsewhere, this is oppression. This disparity was even true after the lottery was instituted. It could be proven by the numbers that LBJ was conducting genocide against blacks and if the press were not left-leaning that would have been done. It certainly would have been blasted out had LBJ been a Republican.

The affluent were able to at least delay the conscription by staying in college, what was called a student or 2-S deferment. Yes, I was one of the 2-S holders, but I started college in September 1961, before the buildup and before my 19th birthday. I was going to college for an education not to defer conscription. Some started or remained in college for the deferment. Some went to college, kept in college, got married, all to maintain the deferment. But they were the rich and privileged. During college they found a benign tumor in my femur that caused increasing pain, something that started during the last year of High School. It did not hit the level of medical intervention till late in my freshman year in college and the cause was not found till the middle of my Sophomore college year when I had surgery to remove it. By the time it was found, I was taking pain pills to function. I graduated in February 1965, was re-classified 1-A and was called for a Selective Service examination. I was one of those who were being 'selected'. Based on that exam my classification was changed to 1-Y meaning I could be called if they reduced the requirements. Many were in that category. I am sure that local boards were paid in some areas to set classifications. Selective service was not by any means a uniform, democratic or unbiased process. The Wilson/Creel monster continued to oppress under the progressive LBJ.

The Democrats were strangely silent on this, even in the Nixon years, but let's remember, had they called the attention to Nixon it may have fallen back on his predecessor who had done the same thing. Nixon got a pass, the only one in his presidency to protect LBJ. Oppressive governments are adept at keeping blame from falling on them and as the press lurched to the left it increased its protection of those who would oppress. Their legacy must be preserved to protect the whole rotten liberal/socialist/communist movement. The first rule is, "Liberals can never be portrayed in a negative light." The second is, "No matter what a conservative does, paint it as bad." The press continued its strange silence on this, but we must remember that it was at that time not critical of anyone who looked left-leaning. Johnson got a pass for the most part except from the war protestors who seemed to be unable to fathom that the men going to Vietnam were for the most part, patriots who were serving their country or draftees who were impressed into service by LBJ and had essentially no choice. These left leaning protestors found it easy to bash the military but failed to lay the blame squarely where it belonged, the leadership if it can be called that, in the oval office. The press accented the military presence but not the political backdrop.

They did not understand or did not want to fathom that a soldiers' role was not to question the motives, just to do their jobs and die if that as their lot. As with every war there were soldiers who went beyond fighting and harmed civilians without reason but for the most part, in this war and in others, American soldiers have for the most part carried themselves with honor, both in protecting the US and in not engaging in wanton killing but the protestors took it out on the soldiers and they and the press made the very few regrettable excesses look like the norm. This left-wing mantra of using the rare occasion to dirty all is back in the attacks on police.

Those of us who have never faced enemy bullets (I haven't) can never understand what happens to a person who does. Although I have never looked carefully at the Nixon handling of the war until now, the number of bodies of American Soldiers fell from 16,000 in Johnson's last year to 11,780 in Nixon's first year, to 6000 and 1200 in the two following years. As bad as those numbers were, and they were bad, they were at least declining. Had Nixon continued the level for those three years, there would have been thirty thousand more deaths, nearly a fifty percent increase in the total death toll.

I will add here that if you want to see something interesting look at the Obama years deaths in Afghanistan and compare them to the George Bush years. Each Obama year generally had more American Military deaths than <u>all</u> the Bush years. But the press that could blame Bush for going there without authorization (which was a lie, he had it) lurched to the left and overlooked Obama when he increased the participation. I can say this. Obama was the second-best black president we have had. You thought he was the first and the best? Nobody could be better than Slick Willie Clinton and he was the first black president.[72] In 1998, Toni Morrison wrote a comment for The New Yorker arguing that "white skin notwithstanding, this is our first black President."

Saying that, he echoes novelist [Toni Morrison] who writes in *The New Yorker* that Clinton "is our first black president. ... Clinton displays almost every trope of blackness: single-parent household, born poor, working-class, saxophone-playing, McDonald's-and-junk-food-loving..." (*The New Yorker*, liberal as the dickens, presumably deplores racial stereotypes.)

Understand it was hard to find something good to say about Clinton, so the press pulled out all the stops to try.

From the Press and Sun-Bulletin October 13, 1998.

Early Twentieth Century Dixie

It began in the late portion of the nineteenth century but flourished in the twentieth. Blacks in America were demoted from the equality that Lincoln envisioned, proclaimed in the Emancipation Proclamation and in fact was being approached during reconstruction. It would be a long and hard road, but the path was marked. Laws can guide but the real

---

[72] https://www.theatlantic.com/notes/2015/08/toni-morrison-wasnt-giving-bill-clinton-a-compliment/402517/

change had to come in the hearts and minds of both the blacks and whites. The end of reconstruction short circuited the change.

The demotion took them to the lower caste. Yes, there was a caste system in the US, and although entrenched and well defined there, it was not just in Dixie. It was more than white and black, it divided whites into po whites, middle class whites and the elite whites, the ones who lead.[73] Although some of this happened in the north, particularly in the more liberal New England Snob areas where skin color was not important, blue blood was blue blood, poor was poor, white or black. White trash was a staple description used by the elite. In some places it was trailer trash. But the aristocracy needed to make those who were not them be shown they were inferior.

Even in back woods Mount Holly Springs, there were snob areas to live in. I can remember being called "the kids from over the mountain." In New England blue blood was essential for snob school placement and advancement. It is interesting that this blue blood preference exists to today while skin color can be a plus in the snob areas. They need to have the "tokens" to show their not bigots but let that one show too much comeuppance and you will see a reaction. To combine the Dixie language with the snob attitude, "it looks good to have a darkie in the group to make us look better." In the less liberal areas of the north people were just concerned about living and building. A man's character, to quote a wise man, was more judged by his honesty and work than by his skin or blood color.[74] Using my family, starting with my grandfather who moved from the farm work to running a business, my dad who moved from a laborer to a manager of a factory, and my sisters and I who had successful professional careers, mobility was possible in the back woods of PA. It took hard work. I could show other families who see the same. Without the Dixie Democrat or Liberal Snobbery things went better. Did I mention, this was a staunch Republican area? The Democrats could have held their county meetings in a phone booth. We would have rented the basement of our outhouse to them.

---

[73] This caste system and its impacts are discussed in my book, "The Balkanization of America."

[74] A rephrase of Martin Luther King's speeches. I call him a wise man.

The bastion of the racist caste system, the center of mass, the deepest and most entrenched abuses were in Dixie. By 1915 blacks were, as discussed in the Woodrow Wilson section of this book, removed from influence in the US government. One of the hallmarks of this was so whites would not be put in the demeaning position of having to report to or work with blacks! Imagine that, the indignity of having to ask a black man to approve your expense account! You might have to work next to a black man or woman. How awful! I have worked with blacks, gone to church with blacks, had black subordinates as a manager, and had to go to a black for expense book approval, a black woman no less. None of that ever harmed me. As an aside. I have never owned a slave. Never had a desire to do so, didn't think I needed one. Didn't think it was right. I have over the years worked with and gone to church with fine black men and women – two have first names David. I consider them among the finest men I have known.

I am sure the black backroom clerks, chambermaids and janitors were retained, that kept the 'darkies' in their proper place. Rules were set that white postal workers would not have to work in mail cars with blacks except in 'emergencies'! Those happened under Wilson who many try to excuse saying he bowed to pressure from the Dixiecrats. I see another side, the northern snobbery. Many other changes occurred with the end of reconstruction and the rise of a generation not under the sanctions was the starter gun for the white aristocracy in the south to begin the return of the negro[75] to the plantation. We must remember that by this time the slavery was illegal but the whites who instituted it and maintained it wanted to ensure that the negro would pay for the comeuppance of even thinking he was an equal. Of course, the po whites were to still be kept in check. They did not have the blue blood that was needed to lead either. Yes, the blue blood concept existed in the south. But remember, the southern aristocracy and the Northeastern Snobbery had one common blue thread, the Democrat party! This attitude toward those who do not have social standing, black or white, still exists and is still prevalent, not only in the south but

---

[75] I will use at times the words of the times to show the contempt that these so-called leaders had for blacks. Please, I am using them to show the bias of the time. I do not normally use these.

also in liberal conclaves like Boston, NYC, DC and Hollywood. It isn't just racist. It is not based only on race. It is based on birth. It is a caste system. It is prevalent in the snob colleges that profess diversity but only practice it where it is a show. They will bring in preferred students from Africa and an American ghetto but exclude very qualified students from blue collar families, white or black. Minorities are only window dressing to make it 'look good' or the ones who 'owe them' and can thus be kept in submission.

Barak Obama is one of those preferred, one with privilege who came from Africa. He was born in Hawaii but was raised in Africa by his father in a family of privilege. He and his father were educated here in the US because of the privilege. No matter what his birth, he is not an American, he is not a black American, he is a privileged, transplanted African, born to and raised in a preferred class in Africa. The upper casts honor the upper casts from other areas. If you look at his handling of the government, it is obvious even if you do not know his lineage. He was not a president to Americans. He was a race baiter and a snob. At the time his dad came as a student, we were not accepting Africans but we were Arabs. His dad came as an Arab, a lie. Obama's whole history is based on one lie after another. I believe this fact about his father is why his birth certificate was hidden. Knowing his father was not proud of his heritage and lied about it could have reduced the black vote that was essential to his win. He used the blacks to get to the White House with a lie, one more example of oppression.

In this I am also going to show where these actions were opposed and most if not all of them were removed by 1970 yet 47 years later Jessie Jackson, Al Sharpton, Louis Farrakhan, John Lewis and others still cite them as if they are in existence today. By doing so they are an oppressive force to the average young black who hears continually that the deck is solidly stacked against him, there is no way he or she will get ahead, 'the man' will not allow it. Now they are telling him through the Black Lives Mater that the police will shoot him for sport. All of these are lies, but he hears this, keeps hearing it and concludes the best thing for him or her is go on crack, get jailed or have a couple babies and go on welfare where the Democrats in government will take care of you and oh, BTW, never vote for any Republicans because they want to line you up and kill you. They will take away your food stamps and Obama Phones. The black Muslims are there to help drag these into their web of hatred and malice that further raises the possibility they will run afoul of the law. Young black men are being killed at a horrific rate. Most are shootings were the shooter and the shootee are both black. It is correctly called, black on black crime.

I deal with some of the forces that are causing that elsewhere but let me state a couple here. One of the occupational hazards of engaging in drug dealing is violent death. Let's be honest, as a percentage of the population, more young black men are involved than any other group with young Hispanics being second. Their chances of running afoul of the law or a hostile element in the drug trade are much higher than white men. I believe the hype of the black leaders and the breakdown of the family by the welfare system are responsible for much of this, not some moral weakness of the young black male. Historically blacks have proven themselves to be good, but every person has a price.

There is a story that illustrates this well. A young girl was propositioned by a dirty old man. "Will you go along with me for a weekend, anything goes for a million dollars?" The girl quickly responded, "Yes." The man asked, "Will you for ten dollars?" She looked at him, "What do you think I am?" He laughed, "We established that, now we are haggling over the price."

The drug dealing has a return that is above the price needed to entice many of all races to engage in it. Young blacks are not alone but the pressures of society and the evil rhetoric of their leaders are helping drive them to engage in this ruinous work.

Recently an ad for a Virginia Senate candidate (Democrat) showed a big truck that was obviously driven by a red neck trying to run over people of color and females dressed in the oppressive garb of Islam. It may be well to note that the rebel flag that was displayed is one that far less than one percent of Republicans would even consider flying unless they knew it would piss off and upset a local coven of liberals. I have considered flying one for that reason, a fifteen by ten foot flag on a 50 foot pole. I might even figure out how to put a fan on it to keep it flapping in the wind. Seeing liberal heads explode is fun. I haven't done it because there just aren't enough liberals nearby to be worth the effort.

Most of the ones who would fly this flag are not skinheads, Nazis, racists or white separatists, they are people who have family roots in the south and that is a part of their heritage. I guarantee that if you tried to strip away heritage from any groups other than white Anglo-Saxons there would be hell generated by these very same liberals who are protesting the stars and bars. How about telling Muslims their beards or the stupid getup they require their women to wear are not allowed? I can guarantee this will create havoc. And the liberals will support them.

Several years ago, a Muslim woman in Florida wanted to have her driver's license picture taken with just her eyes showing. The state's refusal set off a firestorm, but Florida prevailed. I bet I would get less flack from liberals if I flew an ISIS flag than the Stars and Bars. Although I will bash the Confederacy and Twentieth Century Dixie, I am a little considerate of the feelings of American Citizens who have roots in the south, whose ancestors fought bravely to protect what they considered their land, even though I consider that concept incorrect. Many of those brave men were po whites that were fed a crock of crap and didn't recognize it. On the other hand, I am not tolerant if they want to reinstitute slavery or any vestige or variant of it. I am not tolerant of any oppression including women being oppressed by Muslim males in how they can dress, what they can do, no matter if here or in Saudi Arabia. I will mention here, there are some Christian sects that have some female dress codes that bother me too. I have mentioned that to some of them with less than cordial responses. One of my stock statements is, "If my religion depends on what I wear it isn't worth much." I have used it elsewhere, but it fits here. Martin Luther King Jr. said that a man's character should not be measured by the color of his skin. I agree one hundred percent and I don't think he would consider me including the shape of his beard, the length of his hair, the stupid dress and other things should either. I don't like tattoos, but if they are tasteful, I can ignore that. If, however they haver Nazi, Satanic, and other offensive symbolism, I tend to be a little less understanding unless it was inked before the person had a life change. That is something to remember before getting a tattoo. They are darned hard to erase. The one change I would make to King's statement is change man's to person's. Women should be included. I am sure the word man to him meant mankind, i.e. both.

If you are black, I challenge you to read the following paragraphs, do research on the statements I make, verify them, then verify them from a second source, and decide for yourself whether what I say is true. I want to start with a historic item, the Emancipation Proclamation. Most know it was issued by President Abraham Lincoln, few know he was a Republican. You will not hear that mentioned on CNN or PBS. You will not hear that if you have a kook liberal history teacher who teaches history as modified to make liberals look good. You will not also be told that Dixiecrats were southern Democrats, as were well over 98% of KKK members.

If I want to disadvantage a group, blonds, short people, whatever the first thing I want to do is segregate them from the general population in some way. Physical separation is one tactic, but any form of separation will work. What divides destroys. The scripture says, "Oh how good and pleasant it is for brethren to dwell in unity."[76] Unity is not the modern Borg Collective of liberalism where everyone thinks alike. It is living with others, even with their imperfections. I challenge even those who do not believe the scriptures to try to refute this passage. When we 'dwell in unity' our homes and communities our lives are more tranquil and safe. Our neighbors may have different interests and we may not be best buddies, but we care about one another. He needs something I can give or loan, he has it. Unity is a condition of oneness of purpose and caring, not one of a lack of diversity, it is caring one for the other. Some of my best friends have vastly different backgrounds and experiences. I am enrichened by knowing them.

---

[76] Psa 133:1 A Song of degrees of David. Behold, how good and how pleasant it is for brethren to dwell together in unity!
Psa 133:2 It is like the precious ointment upon the head, that ran down upon the beard, even Aaron's beard: that went down to the skirts of his garments;
Psa 133:3 As the dew of Hermon, and as the dew that descended upon the mountains of Zion: for there the LORD commanded the blessing, even life for evermore.

Europe accomplished the division of Jews with the ghettos and ultimately Jews were rounded up and sent to slave labor camps and gas chambers. Allow me to comment that the pogroms against Jews and the ghettos existed in countries other than Germany. Most of Europe was very hostile to Jews. We only hear about Germany. Unfortunately, the Jew's homeland was occupied by invaders, hostile Arabs, mostly Muslims. That homeland was theirs long before there were any Palestinians. Jews were taken into captivity by their enemies several times and finally forced out by hostile actions. Even in Europe they faced oppression. Look up the word 'pogroms' if you want to see oppression gone to seed.

The Democrats in the south took a page from Europe's book of oppression of Jews and segregated blacks from the community in as many venues as possible. They used the courts, presidency and legislature to accomplish this. The article at the right from the Daily Ardimoriete (Ardmore OK) June 13, 1913 tells it well. Whites should be spared the indignity of being forced to work with 'negroes' or be under the orders of 'negroes.' Indignity! Really? 'Not have to serve in the same cars?' Will the black skin rub off? Are they carrying some

Congressman Asks Separation of the White and Negro Federal Clerks.

Washington, D. C., June 12.—Representative Aswell of Louisiana introduced a bill today to separate white government clerks and employes from negroes.

It would provide that while there shall be no discrimination in favor of or against employes of equal efficiency on account of race, white clerks shall not be required to occupy the same office in the government departments with negroes nor be under orders of negroes; and that except in cases of emergency white clerks in the railway mail service shall not have to serve in the same mail car with negro clerks.

infection? The work rules noted here also place black workers at a disadvantage for employment as did some rules to 'protect' women. I worry when laws are passed to 'protect'. There is a connotation that a protected species is not able to work as well as others. Separate is never equal. I will note that Representative Aswell was not a Republican. He was a Democrat. Blacks were not allowed to use certain public restrooms, water fountains, snack bars, and most important,

schools and jobs. I want you to remember here that without exception
every such law restricting blacks was written, signed and enforced by a
Democrat. The Democrat Primary in the south decided who would win.
This is the party that wants whites to confess their sin of slavery,
including whites who neither personally or ancestrally owned slaves,
some whose ancestors were not even here till after 1870, but these
same liberals do not want to confess the sin of their party ancestors
who wrote the laws that returned blacks to slavery from about 1900 till
the middle 1900's. Those laws created the victim status for blacks. A
victim is in slavery. Blacks were again in slavery, the neo-slavery of the
twentieth century Democrats, based on dependency on government
handouts. Worse they continue to assign that victim status to blacks
and are perpetuating this neo-slavery. The only blacks that are not in
slavery today are the run-aways who have escaped the liberal run
plantation of "government protection." They have followed 'the
drinking gourd'[77] to freedom. [78]They have individually signed their own
'emancipation proclamation'. It reads, "I am a free man (or woman). I
will not stay on the government plantation." There is an old joke we
seem to have forgotten and blacks are somehow not seeing it, "I am
from the government and I am here to help you." Anyone with a shred
of common sense knows better but blacks and whites forget it when
they are accepting a government 'handout'. And the "government aid"
has not improved the lot of the average black in America. I know blacks

---

[77] When I research the 'drinking gourd' I find two explanations and although
both make sense, one seems to be more believable to me. There is a Folk song
by the name. This has been questioned by some revisionist historians. I feel it
was likely and do not question the story. The slaves called the Big Dipper
constellation the drinking gourd. If you followed it on your trek you would
head north. If you extend the line of the back of the dipper it crosses the north
star. If you keep heading toward the drinking gourd you are headed north and
to freedom. The other explanation that I would somewhat reject was that
gourds were set at places to guide the slaves to places to get a drink. Mainly
they traveled at night. Gourds hanging on a pole or bush would be hard to spot
at night and would be a place to be staked out to catch run-away slaves. As an
aside, I am not sure that much of the folklore about the underground railroad is
fiction. To have run-aways funneled through points would help those who
would capture and return them. But then, I look at common sense, not
folklore.

are innately smarter than to believe that crap, but their minds have been dulled by the government promises and the hucksters who promote the victim status. Think Jessie, Al, Louis and Barak to mention a few. Until they declare their emancipation they will be on the government's plantation in neo-slavery.

Even with FEMA aid after a disaster the government may be there to help you but there is a price in liberty in taking the aid. And I will agree there are times when the government should be giving aid to the people, and when they should accept it, when they cannot make it without such. Most government agencies are not nearly as benevolent as FEMA! We must weigh relinquishing our freedoms against need. Like Esau in the Bible[79] who sold his birthright for a bowl of pottage and saw it as nothing of value, we all too often sell our birthright of freedom to the government for a handout. God hated Esau and quite frankly, I believe he does not smile upon anyone who sells their birthright, even Americans who sell their legal one. Birthrights have a biblical basis. When God ordains something, he does not see disrespecting it as a good thing. Blacks (as do whites) in this country have a birthright of freedom. For whites and some blacks, it goes back to 1778. For other blacks it goes back to 1864. They lose it when they sell it for the liberal lies of victim status and a government handout.

Although the talk about segregation is always focused on education, there was a pervasive and nearly complete segregation of the blacks from whites in all areas of life. I will be bold in saying that this was bad for whites as well as blacks. Any time a group that lives in the same space is separated from another; both suffer. I am not saying the level of suffering is the same, just that it exists. I cannot believe that some white businessmen would have been better off had they been able to serve black clients on the same basis as whites. Some may have wanted to but were restrained by the laws of the area and social pressure. Let us not blame everyone in the south. A white businessman was not free

---

[79] Genesis 25:34 and Jacob hath given to Esau bread and pottage of lentiles, and he eateth, and drinketh, and riseth, and goeth; and Esau despiseth the birthright.
Hebrews 12:16 lest any one be a fornicator, or a profane person, as Esau, who in exchange for one morsel of food did sell his birthright,

to be color blind, even if he wanted to be. The requirement for separate facilities had to cost them money in investment and lost business. Even the cost of putting up signs and monitoring separation has some cost. One thing for sure, it did not encourage blacks to patronize these businesses. I know the economics of additional sales in many businesses based on the concept of variable margin. Once a business has enough sales to pay the fixed costs, the cost of the property, the building, the equipment, interest, the profit margin of additional sales is often pretty good. I worked in one environment where the variable margin was such that each additional dollar of sales was 57 cents profit. We had to do 200 million dollars of sales to break-even with zero profit but if we sold 220 million we made 20 times .57 or 10.4 million dollars profit! That was heavy industrial and restaurants often have higher variable margins. One local restaurant here offered a dollar off a meal if ordered before 4 PM. It pulled in many seniors who can eat early and save money. Even at the reduced price they made over 50% on each sale, a sale that they would probably not make. Imagine the impact to a white run business that was just breaking even if it could have served 5% more customers who were black. I wonder of any of those whites that pushed for segregation realized that. But their white customers would have had to suffer the indignity of eating with blacks! Indignity!? Maybe both they and the blacks would have grown because of that contact.

I sometimes have sat at a table with someone I wanted to meet. One of those turned out to be the Emergency Operations Coordinator for LA County who was a presenter at a conference I was attending. Without knowing who he was, I asked to sit with him. He nodded and we got to know each other. He used the fact we had breakfast together to show something in the session. He was black, yes, but I picked the table because he was just sitting down so he would not be leaving quickly and because I did not know him. As a person in Emergency Services, I get to know anyone I can, a bad day is not the time to exchange business cards. I doubt he and I will ever work an incident together so that was one plus that did not happen. But there were some good things he shared that he did not in the class. I sat down because I wanted to, then realized later how good that action was for me and it provided him with an opportunity in the session I attended to make a good point. I still use the line he did when I asked if I could sit with him. When I go into a restaurant alone, they often ask the size of my party. I respond, "I am here with all of my friends." What I saw of this man, both at breakfast and in the seminar, his circle of friends is large. The circle that he cares for is large and I am sure they are safer because of him. But I got this experience because he was there and I didn't judge him by skin color.

Just the normal interaction of peoples tends to bring them together unless someone external to the relationship poisons the water. Government is to protect. Those very governments, mostly state and local were the ones that poisoned the water. Protection of a significant portion of their population was stripped away by that government and unfortunately it extended to allowing physical harm. Blacks were killed and the local government did not turn a hand to stop it, investigate the murder or bring the guilty to justice and this happened into the 1970's. Blacks were falsely accused and jailed. In some cases, the local and state law enforcement participated in the assaults. This is government oppression at its highest level.

Look at an extreme case of what happens when people are together, Stockholm Syndrome. We learned that hostages begin to bond with captors believing that there is safety in that. Look at how people bond together when the wind and water of a hurricane or the shaking of the earth are the common enemies. I firmly believe that without the Federal, State and Local Governments' despicable actions to alienate them, the poor whites and the blacks in the south and north would have somewhat bonded more. It may not have a close relationship, but it could have been one where they were mutually supportive. I cite an example here of a group that lived near Mt. Holly Springs PA. Although they were in a backwoods area, not one of the progressive, 'diversity-aware' areas they were treated more equally there than in the south and by the way, without government interference. In fact, some of the issues were caused by government interference. Most of the Gumby family have moved away but the church and cemetery they started is still there. A few months ago, I learned that the church, built in 1868 that was in disrepair since no longer being used in the 1970's has been taken on by local historians to be restored. I passed it some time ago and work is in progress. The cemetery now has an attractive iron fence delineating it.

One of the great philosophers said, "I have never met a man I didn't like." I think I have a bumped into a couple I didn't like but they are admittedly very few. I have not found one who if I were in a leaky lifeboat with, I could not work with to patch holes and bail. Unfortunately, the po whites[80] in the south did not realize it should have been them uniting with the blacks against the leadership who had contempt for both and wanted to keep them apart, pissed with each other, fearful of each other and not willing to make friends so they could remain in control. Together they could have improved life for both of them. The po whites actually were the ones who were in the front lines of segregation while the leaders ordered the actions, the po whites took the risks, same as the third day of battle at Gettysburg. The leaders yelled charge from Richmond and the po whites absorbed the union cannon fire and Minnie balls. In the battle of segregation till the later rounds the po whites took the risks, burning crosses on the lawns of black's homes, frightening and in some cases beating and killing them, sometimes burning the home, all offenses that if taken to task could have put them in jail. Fortunately for them, the white segregationist leadership held the legal system tight enough that charges were very rarely brought, punishment was either avoided or miniscule, and in some cases the law enforcement was present for and involved in the illegal activities. In the later days of the oppression some of the whites were held to account and punished. An example is the men who killed several civil rights workers who were not brought to justice for decades. They were the same expendables as the ones at Gettysburg, the po whites. In addition, laws preventing blacks owning firearms existed in some areas further tilting the playing field against the blacks. Consider the current opposition to the second amendment when seeing this. How long till conservatives are targeted in their own homes by liberals.[81] Look at the violent acts of the Antifa hoards at

---

[80] What the southern aristocracy called the poor whites – have done so since before the War of Southern Rebellion. I use the term to show the contempt they had for these who they hopped up with anti-black rhetoric to get them to face Union cannon balls and rifle fire.

[81] Conservative Rand Paul was recently assaulted in his front yard by a left wing

Charlottsville. The Antifa hoards drew in many good people who acted well beyond what they would have without the agitation. Could this violent group start targeting people in their own homes? The Communist Red Russians and the Viet Cong, the quintessential liberals did that. Had blacks had weapons it would have substantially reduced the enthusiasm for violent acts against them. As I mentioned elsewhere, a well-placed rifle or pistol round in a cross-burner's chest or even one fired over heads can seriously deflate the enthusiasm of a mob. As an aside, the much-maligned NRA opposed those laws, the only organization to do that.

Separate but equal is never a valid concept except in the minds of seven addled headed Supreme Court Justices and those who wanted to use the ruse to keep blacks in bondage.   I have doubts that the lawyers who argued it and those who brought the suits ever considered equality of facilities even a remote possibility. Plessy v. Ferguson, 163 US 537 (1896) was a landmark constitutional law case of the US Supreme Court decided in 1896. It upheld state racial segregation laws for public facilities under the doctrine of "separate but equal". [82] These laws were passed by Democrats. The court decided the state law did not violate the US Constitution on a 7 to 1 vote, one justice was absent. Three of the justices who voted 'yes' were nominated by Democrat Grover Cleveland. A 4 to 4 vote would still have allowed the lower court ruling to stand but with less force and a later state case might have been heard with different results.

The whites in Dixie concocted all kinds of roadblocks to prevent blacks from voting. It was one of the ways they were able to gain the control of the south that was progressing toward racial equality by 1910 and with Plessy and other directives the south was firmly in white Democrat hands by 1930 from governors to dog catchers. Although the actions by the Federal government were significant, mainly Wilson and FDR, the worst came from the local Democrats, the mayors and county officials, and particularly the county Sheriffs who could arrest and imprison. These people controlled the lives of blacks and there was no mechanism of restraint or redress if they violated their legal role. They were

---

radical neighbor.

[82] Wikipedia

generally po whites, but these were beholden for their winning the office to the white aristocracy. Remember this when you go all gaga over a presidential or gubernatorial election, are hot to troop out and vote then and skip the off-year elections and fail to do diligence in voting in the local races. These people control your lives. Look at your local and school property taxes if you doubt me! In most areas of Pennsylvania, nine people whose names you don't know set the school taxes.

Until the 1950's the Federal government was either impotent or a willing accomplice by inaction. The excesses in the south have brought us to the point that today we cannot enact laws requiring ID to prevent voter fraud, something that is done in many other nations. Blacks fear any rule that can prevent someone from voting is aimed at them, and anything that has a requirement is possibly a way to 'suppress the black vote' and the hysteria is augmented by empty-headed or lying liberal firebrands claiming to be advocates for blacks and black leaders; both of which have a vested interest in blacks staying on the neo-plantation and voting for socialist candidates. The black leaders need a cause to remain relevant. Any cause will work. Any common-sense ID requirement is met with cries from the black firebrands and the white left wing, charging that it is aimed at "suppressing the black vote." That almost every black and white voter in the US already has a valid ID and those who do could get one free. In Pennsylvania the stricken law would have provided free picture ID as a part of the law to anyone who did not have one. People without ID's could have gotten them. That law would have had some value for these beyond voting.

But then, unlike the Democrats in the south that wanted to suppress the black vote, the current liberal Democrats know they have the black vote sewed up and want to be sure they keep it. If blacks were to leave the Democrat-run plantation in voting this concern for them would evaporate as fast as a cup of water poured on desert sand. Most blacks already have ID. They need it for many other things, to drive, access government buildings, and get government handouts. All the voter ID laws mandated the state provide one, free. One of the networks did a man on the street on this and liberal whites in snob towns all expressed that ID requirements were only aimed at ending black votes. The blacks all saw no problem, a couple questioned the need, but all were amazed at the concern. Most of the blacks asked, "Doesn't everyone have an ID?" One man offered that if someone didn't have one, the office to get one was nearby. He pointed and said, "Over there."

I will digress here to show the bi-polar nature of the federal government. Civil rights were being violated for citizens during the 1900 to 1952 period and the Federal Government was at best a bystander and often a participant. The basic federal law, the Constitution of the United States was being violated, it was not isolated incidents and the Federal Government stood silent. It is to the Executive Branch to enforce these laws and it failed. The Executive branch was headed by Progressives, Democrats Teddy, Woodrow, Franklin and Harry for thirty four of those 53 years. Sure, the Republicans did not have stellar accomplishments in the other 19 but we must consider, according to Progressive folklore this is expected, they will beat down the little guy. I will also note that the black assistant Attorney General fired by Wilson was appointed by the previous Republican administration.

The article about Negro Federal Officers in the Woodrow Wilson Section of this book blames "the political party that he (the negro) helped keep in power." (The Republicans.) Later it states, "the young negro for the most part is without frugality or industry. He works only when he must and spends his time in idleness when he can." It blames the negro for laziness and the Republicans for advancing him!

Even today the Federal Government can pick and choose what laws are enforced. Removing the Ten Commandments and Confederate flags and statues from public buildings, bathroom rules for a minority and the like can be enforced aggressively while critical items, border security and public safety can be ignored and the Federal Government has stood idle. Governors of Sanctuary States, Mayors of Sanctuary Cities, Police chiefs who fail to enforce the laws and worse, frustrate ICE enforcement, all should be rounded up and jailed as common criminals for conspiracy to violate federal law.

Federal Marshalls and troops enforced integration at Little Rock and Old Miss by threatening governors with arrest. Why not march federal troops into Sacramento and arrest the Governor of a Sanctuary State who is conspiring with others to violate federal law? I would include the mayors of LA, Philadelphia and others in this roundup. I would love to see that perp walk. Definitely, the mayor of the city who warned that an ICE raid was coming should be jailed. She put at least law enforcement at risk and possibly members of the community. A charge of reckless endangerment is not a stretch.

I am an appointed Judge of Elections in York County PA. In that role I am appointed to serve as the person who leads the election at a polling place for which the elected Judge of Elections cannot serve. Several years ago I served at a polling place in center city with a predominately black electorate. This old white guy got some strange looks and some very illegal heckling. The one person, a black woman actually walked in, looked at me and said with a voice that may have been heard the whole way to city hall, "I can see this election is rigged", apparently based on my skin color. She was sure a white guy couldn't do it fairly but then Supreme Court Justice Sonia Sotomayor thinks a Hispanic woman can judge better than a white man. As a private citizen she is entitled to that opinion, but it should have invalidated her appointment to the court. I guess these two didn't hear Martin Luther King's statement that a man's character should not be based on the color of his skin. I am just as sure that King would have included ethnic background in his exclusions had he been asked.

I think I proved my fitness to serve to her when after significant heckling I went to her and quietly told her she could stay, observe, even question me on actions but she had no right to disrupt the polling place. She reluctantly took a seat and was relatively respectful and I did not have her removed, something I had a right to do by her actions. After I handled one situation for a voter who had a problem she disappeared. Maybe I did it right. The most frequent question at the various polling places? "How do I vote a straight Democrat ticket?" I will note that a few whites asked too, maybe as large a percentage of the total. In eight years of this service I have NEVER been asked how to vote a straight Republican ticket and I have served in districts so heavily Republican that the Democrat voters can hold their meetings in a phone booth. I shudder when I think, "This person who does not know how to vote a straight party ticket is voting!" Maybe the southern literacy laws for voting were not a bad idea but only if they were applied uniformly to whites and blacks.

The ancestors of those White Liberal Democrats were the ones who placed many of the roadblocks in the path of blacks voting. Their opposition to any laws may be doing penance or to prevent them from regressing to the sins of their fathers. I might add that both senators LBJ and JFK voted for a voting rights bill before they were elected in 1960 and then a few months later voted for a bill that prevented it being enforced! That either of these two astute politicians with support of their staffs did that in ignorance flies in the face of any common sense. They knew exactly what the bill meant. LBJ was from the Southern Aristocracy, JFK from the ultra-liberal blue blood Northeast. That nearly all blacks have ID that would enable them to vote is ignored as is the fact that they can get a free ID. But the alt-left's agenda will never be hijacked by something as trivial as the truth.

I can remember the bipolarity and flip flopping of the left during the 1960's when all of this was being discussed. Companies were ordered to remove the block "race" from their employment forms. There could be no reference so there could be no bias. It was ludicrous. When the person showed up for an interview, how could race not be noticed unless it was in the forum of a confessional? Admittedly, the application could be pre-sorted with that block, but it didn't matter if someone wanted to discriminate. A two-minute interview could handle it. But on the other hand, removing it allowed those few companies that were discriminating to say, "We don't know how many blacks apply or how many we have hired. We aren't allowed to ask a person's race." I am sure the lawyers who argued that for them crossed their fingers behind their back or their noses grew when they made the arguments. The block was quickly made mandatory. Liberals can strain on a gnat and swallow a camel. They rarely look at the consequences when they have a pet idea. Remember that neither of these rules were by action of elected legislatures, they were rules written by bureaucrats. The alt-left is also noted for jumping to conclusions and cause[83] but that is the

---

[83] The best teaching on problem solving and decision making is in books by Kepner Trego. The alt-left apparently has never read them. There are others

definite result when your pre-conceived notions override solid evidence.

I heard a recording of a black teen in school who told his black left-wing teacher that more blacks are killed by blacks than by whites. She denounced the teen and his numbers. They are FBI numbers, but she asked where he got 'his numbers' even after he told her where they were from. The facts didn't fit her paradigm. Those facts were not relevant. They were to be ignored. As a statistician I would say it was nearly nine times as likely that a black was killed by a white than by another black, and just as likely that the killer would be Hispanic based on the population but FBI statistics that are credible (based on an informal study I did of homicides in Chicago) say it is the reverse. Blacks kill most of the murdered blacks. In about a hundred cases I saw only a few blacks who were killed by whites or Hispanics. I didn't see one killed by an Oriental. Again, this is an informal study, where available the ethnicity was determined by a picture. The ethnicity in some cases (Hispanics where pictures were not available) was based on sir names and that can be wrong. However, the disparity was so great there even if 20 percent were wrong it still would have had the same result. My observations did not contradict the FBI numbers.

A reporter named Robert Lee was denied a spot on an ESPN college game team because his name might offend some blacks. He is of oriental descent and they are not a solidly Democrat electorate. They don't matter. I sincerely doubt he is a descendent of Confederate General Robert E. Lee unless the general was a Democrat and having affairs with Oriental women. Somehow, I think a lawsuit of discrimination because of name is as valid as one complaining discrimination on the basis of race. I would love to see Robert Lee sue the pants off ESPN and live in luxury for this act of idiocy.

On the other hand, if you watch the news you would expect that cops only kill blacks. Statistics show cops kill far more whites than blacks. These killings make local news but almost never make the state or national news programing, so you only see one if it happens nearby. After all, blacks in New York City and more important, the liberals who

---

almost as good that follow the same lines.

select the news stories to run are not interested if a white person is killed by a cop in rural Pennsylvania, even if it is a bad shoot, and we had one about a year ago that never made either statewide or national news. It doesn't make the cut. And more important, that white guy who was shot probably clings to his guns and bible. From the liberal view he is a despicable. We don't have air-time to spend talking about him.[84] The world is better off without him. Note, this is not my thoughts, it is the liberal idea. He may be one of the Perry County Scum Bags that the former mayor of Harrisburg (a liberal Democrat) accused of hauling their garbage to the city and dumping it along the street. I know quite a few of those "Scum Bags". The ones I know could be trusted to hold your keys or wallet and you would find nothing missing when they are returned. If you had a problem, they would work hard to help. They have three flaws. They are mostly conservative Republicans or Libertarians. They work hard, keep their families, and frown on people who don't. Most own more than three guns and bibles and go to church regularly. They are suspicious of anyone connected with the government. They support the constitution, including the first and second amendment as well as the other twenty couple. They will also tell you if they think you don't have it right. They will not bash in your head or try to silence you, but they will tell you if you are full of bull and will not try to be elegant about it. The thin skinned Antifa can't stand that. They will try to bash in your head. I will also mention, they are pragmatic. Why haul your garbage to Harrisburg to dump it when there are lots of ravines in Perry county? I am sure they also know that Harrisburg already has enough garbage.

The Civil Rights act of 1957 and the Civil Rights Act of 1960 were both detailed in the article noted.[85] Wiki is mostly accurate in what it contains but fails miserably with accuracy when it ignores pieces of history to protect liberals. Let's look at the thrusts of these two civil rights bills that were passed under and signed by Eisenhower.

---

[84] WHAT'S TRUE In absolute numbers, more white people than black people are killed in police shootings (because white people outnumber black people in America). Even left-wing Snopes agrees.
[85] Civil Rights Act - Black History - HISTORY.com
www.history.com/topics/black-history/civil-rights-act

On September 9, 1957, President Dwight D. Eisenhower signed into law the Civil Rights Act of 1957. Originally proposed by Attorney General Herbert Brownell, the Act marked the first occasion since Reconstruction that the federal government undertook significant legislative action to protect civil rights.

The Civil Rights Act of 1960 (Pub.L. 86–449, 74 Stat. 89, enacted May 6, 1960) was a United States federal law that established federal inspection of local voter registration polls and introduced penalties for anyone who obstructed someone's attempt to register to vote.

Note the last line in the first paragraph, "the Act marked the first occasion since Reconstruction that the federal government undertook significant legislative action to protect civil rights." I have looked and can find no evidence that this statement is not true. If it is not, whatever was done was not effective.

With Democrats in the White House and controlling the Congress more than half of the time, with the left listing Supreme Court appointed by FDR, nothing legislative was done until 1957 under Eisenhower and again in 1960 under the same president! Let's face it, the president sets some of the tone on what comes out of the sausage extrusion factory called the Congress, but he can only suggest. Ike's understanding of people that made him the success in leading the Allies in Europe in World War Two helped move things in DC. Yes, it took him five years, but the US congress is the opposite of progress. Allow me to explain that. Pro and con are opposites, so are progress and congress. Remember this legislation only came after Ike's actions in the early 1950's to use Federal Troops and Marshalls to integrate education and marches by civil rights groups brought attention to the situation. I believe these actions forced the hand of the Congress. They had to act. Had TR, Wilson or FDR wanted some civil rights legislation, it would have at least been discussed, even if it failed. None of them ever pressed for it. It was never discussed.

We should remember that Ike was in office from January 1953 to January 1961. It is also noteworthy that he enforced school integration both at the high school and college level using federal troops and marshals. It is also well to note that those opposed to this were Democrat governors in several states, Democrat mayors, sometimes backed by armed police and state troopers. One of those governors was George Wallace who was made presidential runs in 1964, 1968 and 1972. In his 1963 inaugural address for governor of Alabama he declared that he stood for "segregation now, segregation tomorrow, segregation forever". He was a solid Democrat. He also tried to prevent blacks from entering Little Rock High School. Federal troops with M-1 rifles with 8 round clips checkmated the State Troopers with short barreled six shot .38 specials. The troopers wisely holstered their weapons. The guard troops were southerners and it is likely that some had pro-segregation feelings but had someone fired, self-preservation would have taken over and the guard had the far superior firepower. Lots of German and Japanese soldiers could attest the M1's power if they had survived it. Many didn't. It was deadly at a distance and more so close in.

The 1957 act was noteworthy because it was the first such action to address segregation and discrimination since reconstruction. Let us view how it was passed. "The bill passed the House with a vote of 285 to 126 (Republicans 167–19 for, Democrats 118–107 for) and the Senate 72 to 18 (Republicans 43–0 for, Democrats 29–18 for)."[86] Had Republicans not heavily supported this bill it would have never become law. Note that not one Republican Senator opposed the bill.

The 1960 act passed the House with 311 to 109 with two thirds of the Democrats voting yes 179 to 93. The overwhelming Republican vote, 132 to 15, insured passage. In the Senate it was approved 71-18. with some amendments. Again, not one Republican Senator voted against the bill. The amended bill was sent to the House and was approved 295-288. Note that the first gross house vote was 311 to 109 indicating that 16 house members changed their votes from yea to nay. This is not unusual in voting and often indicates the defectors could not support a watered down conference bill.

Both bills became law with Ike's signature. Let's see, wasn't he the same party as Lincoln, a Republican?

---

[86] Wikipedia

Some will say that the opposition in the congress was the "Dixiecrats", southern Democrats. Most of it came from them but let us be honest, the northern Democrats voted against some of these bills to get votes for other pet projects. They wanted power more than what was right.

President Lyndon Johnson was able to get the much touted 1964 act passed but not without the active support of Everett Dirkson. An Illinois Republican from the solid Republican middle of the state, not the socialist bastion of Cook County, got a vision of the need and pressed the bill to passage. The bill was bitterly opposed in the Senate. Although Republicans numbered about 30 percent of the legislature, they more strongly supported the legislation, voting over 80% yeas in every key vote. The Democrat Yeas numbered between 60 and 66 percent. The bill may have failed had the Republicans voted as they are pictured.

> The most fervent opposition to the bill came from Senator Strom Thurmond (D-SC): "This so-called Civil Rights Proposals, which the President has sent to Capitol Hill for enactment into law, are unconstitutional, unnecessary, unwise and extend beyond the realm of reason. This is the worst civil-rights package ever presented to the Congress and is reminiscent of the Reconstruction proposals and actions of the radical Republican Congress."

Note that Strom was right. This was in fact the first real civil rights package presented to congress, so it was both the best and the worst. Note that he gives the Republican Congress of the 19th century the credit for the reconstruction that really was the vehicle that freed the slaves. "(It) is reminiscent of the Reconstruction proposals and actions of the radical Republican Congress." Based on what happened when it ran out, was reconstruction really bad? There was no way the Southern Aristocracy wanted return to the restraints of Reconstruction, the legal authority that liberated blacks until it ran out. I cannot comment as to the constitutionality of the law other than to say, it was not successfully challenged in the court, a good indication it did not violate, and it is easy to see that Reconstruction was necessary based on what happened when it expired.

On the morning of June 10, 1964, Senator Robert Byrd (D-W.Va.) completed a filibustering address that he had begun 14 hours and 13 minutes earlier opposing the legislation. Until then, the measure had occupied the Senate for 60 working days, including six Saturdays. A day earlier, Democratic Whip Hubert Humphrey of Minnesota, the bill's manager, concluded he had the 67 votes required at that time to end the debate and end the filibuster. With six wavering senators providing a four-vote victory margin, the final tally stood at 71 to 29.

One must note that Democrat Robert (KKK) Byrd was in fact a member of the KKK and incidentally, eulogized by Hillary Clinton as one of her mentors. It is also well to note that LBJ, a southerner with no stellar record on civil rights was facing an election in 1964 and was on board. It is unfortunate that most laws are written only after there are significant abuses to address. It must get very bad before congress will act. Although there were offenses in the north and west and these should not be trivialized, for the most part the serious offenses that brought about these laws were in Dixie. The other difference in this, the one that is foremost in my mind, in the south much of the discrimination was supported by state and local governments and in many cases were legally mandated. The amassing of power and oppression was more than 'it just happened.' These were systematic, planned and designed to oppress the 'darkies'.[87] <u>The offenses in the south against blacks were not for the most part violations of local and state law, they were the law and were enforced by the authorities who were sworn to serve and protect.</u> These were Democrats. The federal government stood on the sidelines while the constitution was being violated.

I know these occurred on other places. In 2008 I had an opportunity to talk with an awesome lady in her late seventies near Mt. Holly Springs, Pennsylvania. She was

Copyright Ralph Brandt York PA 2012

[87] I sometimes use the terms the people of the era used to show the contempt they had for others.

a black girl who grew up on Mountain Street, also referred to not so affectionally as Smokey Row. I mention this settlement elsewhere. The name had no connection with any smoke but of the dark skins of the residents. I will state emphatically there was some discrimination there. The settlement of blacks had migrated north from Virginia in the late 1860's and settled there. I have no idea why they settled there and farmed. It was not the best for farming, a sandy soil and it was backed against the mountain – hence the official name of the street. As far as I can determine it did not match any of the other places migrating blacks settled. They usually opted for cities. I can tell you that their survival there was a testimony to their hard work, knowledge of farming and commitment.

This community built a church and established a cemetery that is still

there. As an aside several of the graves are marked as Military Veterans. The church is still standing, in terrible repair as of 2014. Not wanting it to disappear with no record of it, I took pictures in 2008 and was afraid to go inside because I was alone and not confident of the integrity of the floor after 38 years of being unused. I took the pictures through a broken window. I remembered Stuart Hamblen's song, 'This Old House' as I took them. The line says, 'I see and angel peeking through a broken windowpane.' Okay, I am far from an angel, but I would not have been surprised had I turned and seen an angel looking over my shoulder, smiling that someone cared enough to record it. The pictures are on the web under my name.

I felt I got a glimpse of a piece of history. Looking at the construction of the church, a tin roof, log construction with siding covering it, I got a glimpse of hard -working people who loved God and each other. Even the construction of the church is a testimony to the commendable character of this group. The bible is open on the pulpit, the organ still there, and even the seats although they have been moved. Other than that and a couple soda bottles on the floor there has been no vandalism. Somehow this abandoned church has been held as sacred to the community. Inside it is much the way it was in 1970 when the last services were held there. This building was an active church for over 100 years. The last pastor lived in the Chambersburg area and commuted on Sundays. She was elderly at the time and had to have someone drive her. I have forgotten the name but when I was told it I recognized the name and knew I was in a service where she preached in a tent meeting at Pond Bank[88] in the early 1950's. I mentioned elsewhere that the backwoods Pentecostals for the most part were open to blacks attending their services or joining them. It went beyond that. The churches I attended never had a black pastor but there were visiting ministers who were black. This lady was only one of the ones I heard. But then, the Apostle Paul said, "In Christ there is no Jew or Greek, male or female, bond or free but we are all one in Christ." The people in these backwoods areas believed that and even if they did not carry it out to the satisfaction of the white liberals, they worked at it. In God there is no black and white either. In the early 1950's, while many

---

[88] Pond Bank is a settlement about two miles south east of Fayetteville PA. It was the site of a sand quarry, Mt. Cydonia and the home of many of those who worked there. The company moved to another quarry site several miles east since 1950. The southern edge of Pond Bank with its small quarry workers' homes is the northern border of Penn National Estates with its elegant near-mansions. When I learned that Brian, a friend lived in Penn National Estates I mentioned that he really lived in Pond Bank. He laughed. "I like most of the people there better than the snobs that live around me." I go to Martin Luther King, "A man's character should not be judged by the color of his skin." I do not believe it is taking too much license to suggest King would not also have included his job, clothing or the size of his home. I think Brian, a southern boy about my age knew that. He was not the problem.

mainline churches were segregated, the backwoods Pentecostals welcomed blacks. Many of them were living out of the segregated church model and not a lot of them broke with the black churches and attended.

Going to the other side, this elegant lady told me when they went to the movies in Carlisle blacks had to sit in the balcony. Her answers were mixed. She was very adamant that they saw little if any job discrimination in the area and she made a point of saying they did not have to step off the sidewalk to let a white pass like in Virginia. She apparently knew of the oppression of her race in the south. I am sure they saw both good and bad in this backwoods area. I hope it was more good than bad.

A couple years later I was in a restaurant in Mt. Holly and handed pictures of the owner's grandfather working in the field to him. He offered me some Carlisle School yearbooks, circ. 1954. They had belonged to his mother, a white girl. One of them was the year the lady I talked to had graduated! He offered them to me. I did not take them but now I wish I had and had somehow turned them over to a historical society. He saw no value in them. The one contained things the woman wrote to the yearbook owner! I am very sure that when the restaurant closed these pieces of history were trashed. He did not understand the value of his birthright.

When I was at the church a man who lived across the street came over and wanted to know what I was doing. At first it was confrontive and I realized he was making sure I was not intent to do damage. He was white, and one who Hillary would have called a despicable red neck, had a pickup truck in the driveway but he was protecting the church like a neighbor should. I told him I was photographing it to preserve the memory and asked if he knew about the church. He said he was glad someone was. His demeanor changed and he then pointed me to 'the really nice black lady who lives in that house.' He pointed to one along 'smokey row.' It replaced the one that I pictured above. That is how I met her. I mentioned that encounter to her and she responded, "I have only met him a couple times." She was somewhat surprised at the kind reference he made to her. You can pick that the 'nice black lady' reference is not politically correct but not the sentiment. He had apparently seen something good in her. She then related to me that one day she started out with her car, the windows fogged, she pulled to the side, a white man pulled in behind her, came up to her car and asked if she needed help. The man lived in a trailer court nearby and knew who she was and was concerned. She felt that was so great that he cared. In spite of color and the back woods area where this happened, people can overcome differences if allowed to work them out. They can care about others and that is really the crux of the whole matter. It may take some time, they may falter in doing it, not use the most politically correct language but it happens. I have doubts that the civil rights laws made a lot of difference in this area. People just worked it out.

I relate this for a reason. Without laws there were some problems in the north. I am sure we did not go out and try to register blacks to vote but I was not aware of any roadblocks to their registration. My dad was a manager at a canning factory. If blacks showed up looking for work, they were hired if there were openings. There was no drive to increase black employment statistics or practice reverse discrimination, but if someone wanted a job, there was opportunity. I am sure there was other discrimination like at the theatre. I am also as sure that, contrary to the popular liberal Kool Aide, blacks in the backwoods and small towns where it was just let happen, generally fared better than those in liberal snob conclaves. I will note that just a few years ago in a liberal snob New England town a neighbor called the police because she was told a black breaking into a neighbor's home. The person was the neighbor who had locked himself out, but she apparently did not recognize him. Whether she had bad eyesight, poor lighting or just didn't know her neighbor is up for grabs. As an aside the guy breaking in got mouthy with the cop, refused to give ID and got taken in by the cop. There were two mistakes here, the neighbor not recognizing him and his refusal to cooperate. Barak Obama weighed in on this without knowing the facts, called it racism and later had to eat crow and later drink beer with the man and the cop.

I am sure Al, Jessie and Louie would find things to complain about what happened in Mt. Holly Springs. On the other hand, I believe the blacks who lived in our back woods area probably had it as well as in the cities and certainly better than in Dixie. One of the bad side issues of these very necessary laws was the mental backlash in areas that did not have the terrible abuses when they were passed. I believe the laws were right. I believe they could have been reported better to the public that they were to stop abuses, primarily legally mandated abuses, and were not intended to give blacks special privileges. This bad context came through some reporting at that time. It was hard for someone in the backwoods north to understand the way blacks were actually treated by law in the south. I know my surprise at the sign on the Roanoke bus. I am sure some said, "Why do we need those laws? We don't do that crap here. This is just more government interference." Where some minor course corrections were valid in the back woods, a U turn was needed in Dixie. I was a junior in High School before I learned about the KKK in a history class. If there was any Klan activity in our area, it was well hidden. The only Klan activity I am aware of in the Hanover, Carlisle and York areas happened in the late 1900's when there was a Klan attempt to recruit in West York. They passed out a lot of literature, but I am not aware of any real activity and recruitment. One of our church members was handed some of that literature. He brought it to the pastor and asked about it, noting that there was considerable use of scripture. The pastor started walking the man through the scriptures and showed him how God's Word was being perverted. I believe the church and community were better for that. One of the best ways to defeat evil is to turn light on the darkness.

Public Transportation in Dixie was segregated. The famous event in this was Rosa Parks who organized a boycott of the public transportation. Public transportation is generally a venture with very high fixed costs and a very tight budget. If the ridership drops twenty or even ten percent, it is a financial disaster. The income drops but the fixed costs continue. The financial ink quickly turns bright red. Rosa hit the system where it hurt, the pocketbook. It brought some reality.

As a ten year old white boy from the back woods of South Central Pennsylvania who had met maybe a score or so of blacks, I was totally confused when I saw signs in a Roanoke Virginia bus that said, "Whites to front, Coloreds to the rear." "Why?" I only saw the sign after I got on the bus, saw this very wide seat in the back and bounded back and plopped on it. Even after I saw the sign it made no sense. Someone was yelling. I realized it was the bus driver, but I had no idea why. The only other person on the bus, a black gentleman with salt and pepper hair sitting next to me leaned over, "Sonny. You need to go up front. He is yelling at you. You can't sit back here. If you do, he will make me get off the bus."

I didn't understand it, but the man was nice, so I went back to the front with my aunt. I didn't understand it, but I would do what the nice man asked. I was still confused. Why did I have to sit in the front? I thought that big back seat was nice. Why couldn't I sit there? I remembered that one night when boarding an aircraft in Harrisburg, I believe a Metro, that had a large bench seat for five people in the back. It reminded me of that man and his kindness. I didn't realize the sign was targeted at the nice man in the back, not me. Looking back, I realize that a ten-year old boy with no training in diversity and race relations had it more together than the supposedly intelligent people who ran the city of Roanoke and the Commonwealth of Virginia. I did not know enough to be a racist. The man was nice. The angry bus driver was not. As an aside, most of the blacks I had seen by that time were people who visited our church. We were back woods Pentecostals and didn't have enough knowledge of blacks to know they shouldn't be meeting with white people. The blacks were people who we knew God loved enough to send Jesus and we were working to lead people to know Him. They believed in Him like we did. It was simple. If they knew him, they were our brothers and sisters. If they didn't know Him, we wanted to make the introduction. Over the years I have seen that if you have love as God has defined it you don't understand some of the things supposedly educated people do. If you want to see how this is defined, see First Corinthians chapter 13.   I will give you the first two verses. [89]

> 1Co 13:1 If with the tongues of men and of messengers I speak, and have not love, I have become brass sounding, or a cymbal tinkling;

---

[89] I used Youngs Literal Translation here rather than the KJV or its derivatives that use the word charity not love. Both words are correct translations, but most Americans understand love, not charity. The 1600 meaning of charity is a very special kind of love, close to the kind of love God has for us.

> 1Co 13:2 and if I have prophecy, and know all the secrets, and
> all the knowledge, and if I have all the faith, so as to remove
> mountains, and have not love, I am nothing;

I have written my own translation of verse one, "No matter how holy I sound, if I do not have love, I am a bunch of ridiculous noise." I do want to remind you; love is an action verb. Often it is doing. If you have not read the whole chapter of First Corinthians 13 in the last year, do so. It is all good.

Dixie, sometimes called the bible belt has ignored the law of love. They have torn out pages of the bible – ones written by John, Paul, and James and quotes of the words of Jesus. How can it be called the bible belt when they ignore significant portions of the scripture? I can give you an answer. They are using the Bible as a whip to beat others. As the Apostle Paul would say, "Brethern, these things should not be."

My mind goes back to a morning at York Christian Fellowship when Pastor Jack Cashman held his bible by one page and it tore. I don't remember what he was illustrating but he taught me something. **He just tore a page out of the bible!** I sat there and realized that we often do that by not believing or by not following what is there.

I can't remember which city but when Oral Roberts was conducting the large tent meetings in one of the southern cities, he designated some nights that were for blacks only. The city had a law that blacks and whites could not have mixed public meetings. Imagine that, this was legally mandated church segregation. This is what I am talking about when I say we need to work to get rid of legally mandated oppression. In one other town (I believe it was Washington DC) there was a marked off section for blacks to comply with local regulations and I might mention, it was not in the back. It was a front to back slice of good seating and it was large enough. It was separate and we know that separate is not equal but Oral tried to make it as close to equal as possible. Take a lesson from that! We may not be able to be perfect but let us work to be as good as possible. If we each just did a little better, it would spread like an infection.

My family followed those meetings and we were surprised that he took that action to segregate. When we first saw it, we had no idea that the city had such an ordinance. Oral asked that blacks not attend the 'white nights' and that whites not attend the 'black nights'. It cut into his attendance, but he wanted the best for the people. The reason was simple. It was not Oral Roberts that drove that, his meetings were integrated and attended by mixed groups pretty much like the surrounding population in other areas. His reason was simple. If blacks attended on 'white nights' they could be arrested. If whites attended on 'black nights' the blacks could be arrested. Oral did it out of concern for the blacks who could be harmed. The city had a law that blacks could not attend meetings with whites and if they did, they were at risk. You and I could debate till the end of time if Oral should have taken another approach, but I feel he did the best with the situations.[90]

I am sure Oral Roberts reluctantly obeyed the law of the land, one I am sure he disagreed with and he stated that, but he did not ignore the higher law, the law of love. He did the best he could for his brothers and sisters in a bad situation. I will comment that the whites in the area honored his request and stayed away on the nights for blacks. They had it together better than the city fathers.

Allow me to go one step further. The race coin has two sides, one white, one black. Those on the other side of the race coin are not any better than the white racists. When Ray Nagin proclaims that New Orleans will be a 'chocolate city' his attitude is no better than the white-sheeted KKK member who burns crosses on a black family's lawn. After people protested the comment including some blacks, he backed off.

> NEW ORLEANS, Louisiana (CNN) -- Mayor Ray Nagin on Tuesday apologized for urging residents to rebuild a "chocolate New Orleans" and saying, "You can't have New Orleans no other way."[91]

> "I'm really sorry that some people took that the way they did, and that was not my intention," the mayor said. "I say everybody's welcome."

---

[90] Oral Roberts: An American Life - Page 446 David Edwin Harrell, Jr. - 1985
[91] http://www.cnn.com/2006/US/01/17/nagin.city/

Do you want to know, 'what ever happened to Ray Nagin?' He was convicted on 21 corruption charges for actions while in office and in 2014 started serving a 10 year sentence in a federal prison. He will not be eligible for release until 2023.

When Farrakhan said Bush blew the levees at New Orleans, a charge he had no evidence to support, he was no better than Governor Wallace who stood in the Little Rock School driveway to prevent black students from attending.

> WASHINGTON — It's become a strongly held belief by some in the storm zone — the idea that the destruction of New Orleans' heavily poor, heavily black Ninth Ward was neither an accident nor an act of nature.
> Dyan French, also known as "Mama D," is a New Orleans Citizen and Community Leader. She testified before the House Select Committee on Hurricane Katrina on Tuesday.
> "I was on my front porch. I have witnesses that they bombed the walls of the levee, boom, boom!" Mama D said, holding her head. "Mister, I'll never forget it."
> "Certainly appears to me to be an act of genocide and of ethnic cleansing," Leah Hodges, another New Orleans citizen, told the committee.
> Similar statements, sometimes couched as rumors, have also been voiced by Louis Farrakhan, leader of the nation of Islam, and director Spike Lee.[92]

Although not totally correct, when you see the term, Community Leader, think self-serving rabble rouser, troublemaker, fomenter of riots. It wasn't so at one time but the power they have has corrupted them. As for Louie and Spike, I feel definite compassion for someone who is so steeped in hatred that they can create such lies.

When Obama indicted a cop on national TV without any evidence and worse, it turned out to be wrong[93] he was no better than Woodrow

---

[92] Were the Levees Bombed in New Orleans By Lisa Myers & the NBC Investigative Unit updated 12/7/2005 8:38:47 PM ET
[93] Courier Post (Camden NJ) July 30, 2009 Page 6. Gates Caller: Tape Shows I'm not a Racist,

Wilson who fired blacks in the government. When we give one side or the other a pass, we are part of the problem. Anything we do to create more ill will is bad. Peter, Paul and Mary talked about "I would ring out the love between my brothers and sisters, all over this land."[94] I have promised I will do that. Unlike most liberals, I will call a pig a pig, crap, crap, and I will also call racism what it is, no matter if it is being spouted by someone with white or black skin.

When Donald Trump blamed both sides for the violence in Charlottsville he was blasted because the one side was liberal, left wingers. In the mind of the Lefties they could not be the cause. They believe their poop doesn't stink and they don't mind telling you it doesn't. And it isn't all blacks who are the race baiters, Hillary threw in the race card along with the gender card, one that is no less destructive, several times during the 2016 election and even more since. She just can't accept that she lost because people don't like her and she calls Trump a narcissist. I could go on, but the race baiters are there on both sides. Unfortunately, the blacks involved learned well from their white counterparts. Like most issues, neither side in this is any better than the other. Neither have the moral high ground. Both sides are in the mud with the hogs. And they both come out of the mud and hog excrement smelling as bad as the hogs.

North Korea

The difficulties between Korea and Japan are discussed in the section on Imperial Japan. The situation in North Korea was fueled by the same communist expansionist influence that brought about the war in Vietnam, Castro to power in Cuba and several other nations with terribly oppressive governments including dictatorships in South America. The rebels looked to the USSR, got help and used it to out-Communist Stalin and Khrushchev. The inability of the UN forces to stop the communist hoards of North Korea and Communist China left

---

[94] Although the Peter, Paul and Mary cut is the best known it was first performed in public by the writers, Pete Seeger and Lee Hays on June 3, 1949. It was first released by the Weavers in 1950, https://en.wikipedia.org/wiki/If_I_Had_a_Hammer . If you want to see some awesome singing, check out the Weavers.

Korea divided and the north in the hands of a family that has produced some of the most oppressive dictators in history. American policy against communism has been fraught with ineffective use of diplomatic and military power. The North Korean government is toxic. Even family members are at risk if there seems to be any threat to the person in power. Internally the Kim Regime is brutal. Even Communist China has those who dissent. They are dealt with harshly. In Korea there is no dissent because it is dealt with brutally. Even a possible threat to power is at risk. One of Kim's half-brothers was killed outside the country and it appears it was at Kim's bidding.

It seems that when a country is willing to oppress its own, it is willing to oppress others. For years Kim and his predecessor have staged massive amounts of long range artillery and ammunition just north of the DMZ, with millions of South Koreans within their range. Kim is now into rockets and nuclear weapons. Whether he has or does not have nukes at this time is open to question. (The likelihood has increased since the first edition was written.) He does have rockets that are capable of carrying them to neighboring lands. A recent rocket is thought to be able to hit most of the United States. It is believed the payload broke up on re-entry to the atmosphere, good but at some point, the engineers will solve that problem. Heck, it is possible that Obama sold them technology to solve that like Gore sold missile technology to the Chinese that they shared with the North Koreans.

There is also enough engineering data on this that is public to help them. Peoples within the range of those rockets live with some concern. We only have to look back a few years to the Iraqi scud missiles fired at Israel to see an example. Kim has been able to oppress people as far away as the US. I have more concern that he will launch a nuke than I did a Russian launch at any time during the cold war except maybe the Cuban Missile Crisis. I was not as concerned that the Russians would launch as I was that Castro would take those missiles by force and use them. Let's face it, a concerted effort by his forces to take control of missiles in Cuba would have had a high likelihood of success. Although they were under the control of and guarded by Russian troops the numbers of them versus the number of Cuban troops could have forced the issue. A small concerted attack can generally succeed. Could a Russian technician been convinced by threats to fire them? If a single ten-megaton weapon hit Atlanta, Miami, New Orleans, the death toll would have been at least ten times Hiroshima. Think a million deaths per shot. The fission type, atom splitting, weapons of World War II had yields measured in Kilo (thousands) of tons of TNT. They were between 16 and 20 KT. The weapons now being used are in the ten-megaton range. A ten-megaton weapon would be 500 times the power of a 20 kiloton.   I am sure that the rockets Kim has are not as accurate as American and Russian weapons, but then they say, "almost only counts in horseshoes, grenades and nuclear warfare". A near miss on a major city could have 75% of the casualties of a square hit. Even a hit in a rural area would have significant numbers. Kim is a threat.

One of the problems with doing something with Kim, aka Little Rocket Man is simply this. We have, by inaction allowed him to build a conventional army with lots of heavy artillery within range of massive South Korean population centers. These are really hostages. The only way to isolate this is to evacuate these centers, something that is impossible. If this massive amount of firepower were unleashed, it could result in a loss of life near that of a single weapon nuclear event depending on how quickly and effectively the guns could be knocked out. If I were in Seoul, I would be looking for a solid shelter near my home and work.

For those who do not appreciate this. The much-touted Paris Gun of World War I fired about 350 shells and killed about 250 people and wounded 650 more. It fired a 216 mm shell that weighed 106 pounds carried only 14 pounds of explosive. Kim has enough guns of 170 and 240 mm to place thousands of shells a minute on Seoul. Current US munitions in the 155 mm class, and Kim's would be somewhat larger, weigh 100 pounds and carry 23 pounds of explosive. The extra explosive combined with the thinner case would result in more fragments, greater blast distance and more casualties per round. Also, he has had time to target specific points while the Paris gun was just dropping shells somewhere. I am sure the first rounds will be dropped where the population density is high. Artillery fire is an awesome killer. If armor piercing rounds are used on hardened areas like shelters, they too can become death traps.

Kim has oppressed his own people as well. They live in a government-controlled state. There is no freedom and the demands of his military have put the average citizen on an austere life style.

The Obama Regime

The Obama Regime took the US government to new lows in its eight years. He talked about civil rights for gays, lesbians, trans genders, a small minority while ignoring the rights of many. I do not propose any rights be violated, but a president is a president of the whole country, not some small special interest group. Whether the oppression was at his direction or not, he placed people in power who were willing to abuse that power. There was the Eric Holder program, Fast and Furious that had gun dealers make illegal gun sales. I firmly believe the idea in Holder's mind was to entrap the gun dealers and make a show of how they were doing something wrong. The gun dealers played along but were careful to document what they were doing and at who's direction and sidestepped the bullet meant for them. Unfortunately, at least one border patrol agent was not able to sidestep a bullet fired from one of those guns and he was killed. At the best, Fast and Furious was a misconceived idea. I personally believe there is enough evidence to show it was an assault on the liberties of Americans by attacking the Bill of Rights. You will ask, "An assault on the Bill of Rights?" Yes. Let me be clear. An assault on any right of any person or any right is eventually an assault on all. It is why I am so adamant that no right for any citizen be abridged. Although I will bash the defense lawyers for presenting arguments that are so convoluted that no one in their right mind would present it, each defendant has the right to the most effective defense. I do reserve my first amendment right of free speech to call the lawyer a sleaze bag, dupe of the criminal, liar or an idiot when I feel he crosses the line from effective defense to idiocy or dishonesty. Again, I will state, every defendant has the right to have an effective defense.

The targeting of Conservative non-profits by the IRS went well beyond anything that was legal. Someone should have gone to jail for that including but not limited to Lois Learner. This was a concerted effort to silence political dissent, reminiscent of like programs in Nazi Germany. The radical left knows well that money is needed for any political action. The actions to stop dissent were in the form of audits, re-audits, delay in granting non-profit status, and a host of other methods that were just plain wrong. The Tea Party or any ancillary group and Christian groups were the targets. Had this program been aimed at the NAACP, ACLU, or some other left leaning group by a Republican administration, the left listing press would have reported it daily. The Communist News Network and NBC would have been making special reports every five minutes. But they didn't because it was Conservatives that were being blasted and in their minds, Conservatives deserved to be harassed by the government. Did you see the ACLU filing briefs on it? The bias meter goes off scale! The press was in bed with the administration. They are now paying for that with deplorable ratings. As an aside, CNN made its rise on the Gulf War, by reporting it as accurately and timely as possible. People in areas where the cable did not carry it, pressed to have it added. CNN has abandoned truth, accurate reporting and balance.

But Obama went further. In his later time in office he courted gays, lesbians and transgenders to the extent that there was oppression of those who for various reasons find these something they cannot support. I do not see a problem with a post-op transgender guy who now has the physical properties of a girl using a women's restroom or shower or a post-op transgender girl who now has the physical properties of a guy using the men's restroom or shower or if they use the imagined gender restroom and are discrete. If you want to see the idiocy this has brought, here is one.

I didn't make this up. This sign is at the door of the second-floor rest room at the Conference Center at Penn Central College. A significant amount of money was spent to restructure this restroom about 3 years ago, aka Obama idiocy time. The old modesty panels were taken out and replaced with ones that go from just above the floor to nearly the ceiling. There are doors that are very high and they have signs, "urinal" and "toilet". These are not standard, so the word to describe this is expensive. Just the sign probably cost a couple hundred dollars to get it and install it in place of one that said, "MEN". I would be surprised if this "essential renovation" cost less than$50,000. Couldn't this have been better spent on real education needs? How many times does this kind of insanity happen? I will answer that, too often.

Allow me to be crass, it would seem sensible that the plumbing in the restroom and in the person's crotch should match. I would not object to an adult pre-op using a "imagined gender" restroom if they were discrete and dressed as the gender but I have some concern for that in schools. Let's face it, if the person used a stall, I am not going to look over the panel to find out what plumbing they have. Even in the adult areas there are many things that can go wrong and that magnifies in schools, particularly in the middle schools. I know for this I will catch hell from those who are so open minded that their brains have gushed out. I find it totally idiotic to think that a 14 year old who is going through puberty and is as messed up as they generally are being sure he or she wants his or her body irrevocably modified. And I might add, some of those who were modified at a young age are now considering going back, something that is even more difficult than the first transition. Once organs are removed, going back is really impossible. In both transitions there are irreplaceable parts that go to the incinerator. Unless an FTM freezes eggs or an MTF freezes sperm, there is no possibility of genetic children. Despite the hype to the contrary, satisfaction is generally not there with the first surgery. To call this idiocy is to grossly understate it. I could make a case for the argument that the radical left is working to destroy the US, the family, freedom and us as individuals. I have seen the stories of several of these young transitions who are now 'de-transitioning.' It isn't pretty. The ones that are not totally devastated are the ones who have decided to de-transition before they have 'bottom surgery.' YouTube just recently banned a video by a guy who transitioned to female when he was very young and is de-transitioning. It was hateful to say that young people should not be transitioning.

I think any psychologist who signs off on that for someone under legal age (21) should have his license to practice revoked and any surgeon who performs the surgery should face the same punishment. The psychologists should be looking for what got scrambled in the patient's brain and working to help them unscramble it, at least as a first treatment. I have serious concern that many in the LGBT (not all, understand) who claim to be helping youth are actually 'recruiting' and are probably engaging in illegal activities, call it sexual misconduct or sexual abuse. The appropriate action by government is Megans. The Obama regime with direction from the top pushed to allow anyone to use the bathroom or shower room of their choice. This has now cost schools money to refit restrooms and locker rooms, money that could be used for real education needs. Much of the diversity training takes away more money and classroom time. We don't have an excess of either.

I have several experiences that make me sure this is not a good idea. One is the shower rooms at South Middleton Township High School in Boiling Springs, PA. I envision a 14 year old, pre-op transsexual female to male coming in with female anatomy in the buff. Even the changing area would have been a problem. I don't see the pre-op male to female in the female facilities as any better. It is a bad environment for the transsexual and the others there. I do not see how this cannot possibly be a better situation than that person being in the area where the plumbing matches no matter what is screwed up in their head. I will add that in too many schools gender harassment is all too prevalent, and it was when I was in school. Are you trying to tell me that a pre-op transsexual will be better off in the imagined gender shower room than in the one that matches the plumbing? If you are, my statement is, "idiot".

In addition to the opening to someone <u>doing</u> something wrong this opens the door wide to even incorrect interpretation of actions that could result in a real serious issue. If a pre-op MTF in a girl's locker room did something that was wrong, would the liberal minded administration treat the situation seriously. If that same pre-op MTF did or said something that was falsely considered inappropriate could it be used to destroy that person? If some girl said something that is considered questionable, would she be punished. I am darned sure she would. The same issues exist for a pre-op female to male in a guy's locker room. This opens the door to a lot of issues and I am sure there are ones I have not considered. The addleheaded on the left have either not given this much thought or have dismissed the possible, actually likely bad outcomes. Maybe in their minds, these are not bad outcomes. After all, Bill Clinton thought having oral sex with an intern was valid.

The second thing that impacts my thinking was a woman who was taking her male child to a restroom and walked into the men's restroom at a TGI Friday's. She apparently had no concept of the design of male restrooms and worse, the room layout stunk. The doorway was next to the urinals that had no modesty panels so when you came in and turned 90 degrees to continue your path into the commode area you had a full side view of a guy at the urinal. I was there when she entered. I would have expected a fast and quiet retreat. She did the retreat but what she said blew me away. Her exclamation was, "Well I'll be," like I was doing something wrong. I thought an "I'm sorry," or no response to be appropriate. I will admit the experience was bad for both of us, but it wasn't my fault, it was her mistake and she was helped by a bad room layout. I should have probably pitched a fit with the management and sued their pants off.

I see many openings for problems but to satisfy the few, the many must adapt. I will make a crass comment. I recently saw pictures of the 'surgically manufactured pseudo-male equipment'. Knowing what the real thing looks like I am not sure I would display that proudly. I can't imagine going through the surgery and pain to get that even if I lost the equipment I have. I think the risks of a transplant are also too great.

Although I am not convinced of the validity of gender dysphoria, whether it is real or imagined, I have some feeling that those who claim it should be treated properly. This does not include paying for their surgery or hormones, catering to their every whim, or bowing to the current complete idiocy but it does include some sensitivity. What I see as a solution to this is more 'family' type restrooms where those in transition can be in private or at least, allow those to be careful to not embarrass others. And I do believe they should be sensitive to the feelings of others; this applies to the homosexual community too. They would get more consideration from others if there were consideration in reverse. I don't agree with your lifestyle, I see it as perversion. But I will let you follow it and not object if you avoid pressuring me to condone it or rub it in my face.

If gender dysphoria is real, legitimate cases of it would fall on my spectrum like the girl who had a badly deformed leg. The prosthetic for it was not good. She was a champion downhill skier. She wanted the leg amputated and the doctors agreed she would have more mobility. Her parents objected and since she was a minor; she was denied the procedure. She committed suicide.

The big problem and impediment to this is the whole attitude of the vocal portion (but not all) of the gay, lesbian, transgender community, "You have to accept us" and the willingness they have to ram it down our throats. What I really gag on is the "you have to validate our perversion." I look at how I view members of that community I know personally. The ones who do not flaunt their status are ones I respect. They want to live as they want to live, my opinion of them, my accepting them doesn't matter to them. Ironically while I have contempt for those who flaunt the situation, I respect those who just quietly live their lives. I was in a professional setting with two women who were alleged to be lesbian loves. I never checked their intimate time so I cannot say it was true, however there were some indications that was the case. It became an issue one time, brought up by someone as a concern. It was dismissed. These two women were great in their jobs. It would have been better if that relationship had not existed, but it was not a problem.

A good portion of this is based on these knowing what they are and having a good self-image. Ironically because they are not demanding my acceptance, they get at least acceptance as a person. On the other hand, there are some I have known who want me to bow and genuflect to their cause and treat their lifestyle as great and desirable. The former I consider friends and would to a degree support their being what they are in spite of my aversions to it. It is interesting to me that most of the ones I know who are lesbian fall into the former category, most of the gay males the latter. I don't know if this is overall or just the sampling I have. To the latter that I consider oppressive problems, I say, "Get off your high horse." It is unfortunate that these have the support of the government. Like the founders of this country, I reject any oppression from any quarter. The tea gets dumped. Unfortunately, the Obama administration pushed this down our throats.

The worst things the Obama Administration did were in the area of working to incite a race war. We are now seeing this effort come to fruition. I came to the conclusion that he actually wanted blood to run in the streets. You may scream at that but statements like, "Travon Martin could have been my son," and the ones about the cop who arrested the breaking in college professor did nothing constructive and served only to raise racial tensions. His comments about names on buildings and roads, the Confederate Flag and Confederate statues were just plain garbage. They have caused both government and citizen actions that have negatively impacted others. At Charlottesville it resulted in three deaths, three too many. In addition to the oppression, has anyone thought of the impact of changing the name of a college, a building, a road, etc. Remember if you change the name of a road, every person and business along that needs to change their address. For the individual it means dealing with changes to address including driver's license, voting information (called voter suppression?), and other official documents. As an aside, changing your address on a driver's license in Pennsylvania costs money. Who absorbs that hit? The millionaire liberal doesn't see a big ding on his 5 cars, but the average Joe sees a significant ding to change his two. The oppressors don't care about the middle class. These oppressors who want to change history don't care about the tax money spent to change the name on the building, the street signs, money that would be better spent in other ways. I just saw a city school in Harrisburg change its name. That will cost the district at least $50,000. Signs have to be changed, old letterhead and documents discarded, uniforms discarded, anything with the name has to go. And on a sour note, the private, city and state money spent repairing damage, policing and cleaning up after those riots would be better spent on other things. And let me be crass, when property damage, terror, and injury are involved, they are riots not demonstrations. They are no longer protected assembly. If the cleanup is no more than emptying more trash in trash cans, picking up small quantities of carelessly discarded trash, or even collecting the trash around a receptacle that overflowed, that is a demonstration and a valid exercise of freedom assembly. Just remember in dealing with me I am one of Hillary's despicables. Don't expect a lot of concern for crap from me. She has told me I don't have it. I am just living up to her expectations. I am one of Barak's bitter Pennsylvanians who cling to my guns and bibles.

The Clintons

The Clintons have been an interesting group.

As I write this I find there is one conservative, Roy Moore and one RINO, GHW Bush, and a gaggle of lefties including Franken, a bunch of entertainment members and some news reporters, all of these with a couple exceptions are lefties, all under scrutiny for abusing women. Somehow Clinton has escaped the scrutiny but remember, Hillary was guarding his rear. Well, maybe it was other parts of his anatomy. Want to make me laugh, tell me Hillary didn't know about Bill's bimbos.

I find the most virulent abuser of women has been none other than Hillary Clinton. I can't say she has ever sexually assaulted a woman, but she did abuse them and her protection of Slick Willie's willie escapades has can be called nothing but abuse. My argument on this was supported by a recent statement by Monica Lewinski. In it she said clearly that the sex with Bill Clinton was not abuse, it was consensual. Bill lied that he did not have sex with her and Hillary tried to cover it up, like she did with other women. I will deal with that later. She went on to say that the real abuse came later at the hands of those who would protect a president by painting her as the person who was wrong. Although there were many others involved, all we know about this indicates Hillary had much to do with the bimbo management program. Although I do not believe as some did that Bill should have been impeached, I do believe he should have resigned or better fallen on his sword, but unlike many other presidents, Bill had never served in the military and didn't have one. I have had a perverse thought, maybe one of the Marines could have loaned one to him. Anyone with any character would have resigned. That says something about Bill. The people around him would have, had they had character, called for his resignation, not justified his moral depravity, likewise the people of his party. But they realized that if Bill resigned, they were riding a lame horse named Al Gore. Proof of that was a seriously inept candidate,

GWB defeated him in 2000. They would not risk losing power for the good of the country. If you were not around when this happened, Slick Willie, appropriately named, had a 22 year old intern sucking a cylindrical private part of his body. That is an explanation of the polite term and left-wing acceptable act, 'oral sex.'

The left has so often blasted anyone who questions one who accuses someone of sexual assault as putting the victim through another rape but here we have one of those who does not claim to be a sexual victim now say she was victimized by those who needed to keep Clinton in office. I submit that one of these was in fact Hillary who even then had visions of ascending to the presidency in the future to bring the Clinton dynasty to fruition. I am surprised that Al Gore survived the 8 years as vice president, but his ineptness guaranteed his safety. If during the 2008 primary campaign, there had been an attempt on Obama's life I would have considered Hillary to be a suspect. If I were to be a witness against Hillary, I would be packing the largest portable cannon available, possibly two of them, full time and have that loaded weapon on the nightstand. I would have someone else tasting my food. Although initially I saw the "Clinton Death List" as a right-wing attempt to smear her, the more names that get added, the more I reject the bias. Each of these could have harmed the Clintons. Each of them died under some curious circumstances. Some of these are conspiracy theories, no better. Some are very questionable. But when there is a large quantity of smoke, there is no doubt that there is some fire there. If Hillary is responsible, even in an ancillary way, for just one of these bodies she should be brought to justice. Donald Trump said it, "Lock her up."

When I heard Monica's statement the chant at the Trump Rally came back, "Lock her up." At that time, I considered it a rallying call for Trump voters. Now I wonder. Is it what should happen? Right now, I cannot say, "lock her up" without due process. However, I believe investigation and due process is long overdue. I believe if justice were done Hillary would spend some time behind bars for her actions on Bill's bimbos, the election excesses that took out Bernie, Uranium 1, Bengazi, and the Dossier that she funded on Trump, mishandling classified data, et. al. I might add, if they had to lie to get things on Trump, maybe that is an indication that they couldn't find something real. Every time I think about this the statements, "Hillary behind bars", "Hillary in stripes" take on a nicer ring.

Let's go back a few years, to the office of the First Lady in the White House. In 1993 Hillary occupied that office and lo, in it there were found about 50 FBI files. Confidential files about Americans had somehow found their way there. Possibly they crawled there on their own? Maybe they were left there by the previous first lady. I was surprised that Barbara Bush was not blamed by the left for leaving them. After all, everything was "blame a Bush." I am surprised the Clintons or Obamas didn't cut down the rose bushes at the White House in an effort to de-Bush it. What official investigation would the First Lady be doing? She wasn't even a second-rate hack lawyer, slightly better than Michelle Obama. At least Hillary did not surrender her law license to stop an investigation into her activities. What valid reason would she have to be in possession of them. There are also corollary questions that are just as important. How did she get them? I am sure she did not go to the FBI office at night, break in and take them. Someone removed them from the FBI storage and brought them to her. Who was that and why did they do it? Why were they not disciplined or jailed? This was a blatant breach of confidentiality and privacy and nobody was ever brought to account, including Hillary. The current FBI abuses in the Russia debacle are not new. There were investigations of Martin Luther King and others that were not valid. J. Edgar Hoover may be gone but the FBI has not been de-Hoovered. It still is investigating loyal Americans.

The Left listing press spends hours each day on the Trump-Russian collusion. To date nobody has produced any evidence of this and the indictments the Muller probe has made are for crimes outside that venue. But they refuse to discuss Hillary's actions in freezing Bernie out of the primary. The head of the DNC who took over after Debbie Wasserman-Schultz resigned has written a book about this. Note, she is a Democrat who is charging Hillary with crimes! Her mishandling of secret memos, the illegal e-mail server, collusion in the Uranium 1 deal, and lying to congress and the FBI could keep her in jail for years. If a conservative woman had half those infractions she would be in jail.

Martha Stuart committed one crime and saw the world from behind bars. Why isn't Hillary looking through bars?

The Nation of Islam

Although I have covered Islam and discussed the black leadership elsewhere, the Nation of Islam deserves special attention. If anyone in Islam were to carefully look at the activities of Louis Farrakhan they would probably sue him to not use the name. This man is a hate filled, anti-Semite, anti-Christian, anti-US, and probably anti-everything except himself and his finances. But then, that also describes Islam. Any black leader who connects with him taints his own moral ground. I recently heard a black pastor say that Farrakhan did good things and he would work with him. I will remind the reader that people noted that under Hitler, "trains ran on time." I ask, "Does that undo all of the bad?" Does a certain number of 'attaboys' wipe out a certain number of 'aw shits'?

The ACLU and Fellow Travelers

It is a high-sounding name, the American Civil Liberties Union. But when you have the word union it brings to mind the thuggery of the dockworkers and teamster's and how the "public service unions" (includes government workers, teachers, etc.) have corrupted this country by doing anything but public service. "Public Service Unions" serve the union first, the public service workers second and the public third. And the ACLU is less than a notch above the worst of these.

Please don't get me wrong, unions improved the lot of the American worker in their early years. And the ACLU has taken on and won some cases that have been good for the country. Over the years the ACLU and the unions gained power and power corrupts unless men have strong laws to restrain them or strong internal moral compasses. Too many have moral compasses with de-magnetized needles. With the free rein that the unions have had since the NLRB was instituted under FDR things went sour. The Jim and Tammy Bakker scandal, the Penn State Sex scandal, the Olympic Gymnastics scandal, and the Catholic Priest scandal show poignantly that many do not have that compass even in the halls of religion and academia where we would think we could expect better.[95] The diversity of them shows the ease with which a person can be enticed to go wrong. I will comment that I expect other scandals to come out in the open from the sports machines of academia and the entertainment industry. Since the book was written there is another scandal that is just now emerging, academia selling its soul so to speak to the Chinese Communists. One professor in a prestigious University was taking $50,000 a week from the CCP to provide research data.

If there is anything we should have learned from this is that large and rich bureaucracies, no matter in what discipline, see the need for sweeping bad things under the rug and are adept at hiding wrongdoing. They have the money to make it so. The power all too often went to the heads of the leaders. All too often they can find willing accomplices to do so for money or power. All too often when the infraction is minor exposing it would stop the practice and may save both the perpetrator and the future victims pain.

John L. Lewis called a strike in the middle of World War II and defied President Roosevelt. One of the ironies here was the National Labor Relations Board that FDR created was the government agency that supported the strike and it was approved by his hand-picked lackeys on the supreme court. Other union actions have brought violence. Public employees' unions are a major factor in spiraling education and government costs, aka tax increases. That those who hold positions of public safety, police, fire, garbage collection, can strike is a travesty as are those who provide critical infrastructure, communications, power, gas, etc. That government workers unions can spend union dues as campaign contributions, aka bribes to lawmakers to get pay increases is also a travesty. And the ACLU has gained power and it has gotten to the point that they will destroy people over trivia. But after all, they are lawyers and how often has the legal profession ever been validly accused of having common sense or compassion? Yes, it happens, but so do total solar eclipses. The word American in their name plays on the idea that they subscribe to what is American. That is a bare faced lie. They have been responsible for taking prayer out of schools, the ten

---

[95] At the time this section was being edited we had the Hollywood, entertainment, political sex scandals of Harvey Weinstein, Al Franken, et. al. They only serve to underscore the statements made in the text.

commandments out of the public buildings, crosses out of the public eye and killing about fifty million[96] babies in the womb. Only a few despots have been responsible for that number of deaths. They have been instrumental in rulings that have released criminals on a technicality who went on to harm others. In the case, Benitez v. Mata the American Civil Liberties Union obtained the release of Mariel boatlift people because the government could not process the massive influx fast enough. If the government was purposefully stonewalling, I would have supported action against the government, but not just blind releases. And it wasn't stonewalling, it was a volume of work that exceeded the ability of the government to handle it. This resulted in the release of criminals into the US, some of them common criminals who had been hardened in Cuban jails. Many of them were not political prisoners or common refugees. Castro dumped many really bad people on our shores and the ACLU helped free them. They did not delay in going out and committing crimes. Say, "Thank you, ACLU."

The ACLU has school boards and other government entities living in fear of them drumming up some cause and bringing a lawsuit, so they toe the liberal line. One of their lawsuits has opened the door for any juvenile who was sentenced to life to get another sentencing hearing. The lawyers get rich on this kind of thing. We just had such a hearing in Lancaster for a woman who as a 17 year old killed a schoolmate who was apparently a romantic rival. She killed a rival over a guy. It was premeditated, she took the guy along to kill the girl and he helped. It was a vicious stabbing. She will now be up for parole in 3 years. Say, "Thank you, ACLU."

---

[96] The number of abortions has dropped a little in the last ten years, but it was running over one million for some time. Row v Wade was in early 1973, by 1974 the abortion mills were up to speed with just over a million. We now have 44 years of abortions. When you look at four kids born after August 1973 there is one aborted.

Many of the school shootings have been carried out by people who have serious enough mental illnesses to not be able to buy a weapon but court rulings, many argued by the ACLU against the reporting people with mental illness to the government data base have limited the reporting. Seventeen families of dead children in Florida repeat after me, "Thank you ACLU."

And of course, they are behind the transgender bathroom use idiocy. Remember, like the activists in any area, they need a cause to be relevant. They will manufacture one if there is not one available. Currently the gay marriage, LBGT 'rights', Illegal immigrant rights, and the supposed persecution of Muslims will work to stir the pot. Say. "Thank you, ACLU for your efforts to destroy America."

Biased Media

Bias in the media is a serious issue. It has been since the 1930's when the Pennsylvania State Police were operating a radio station that used the same frequency as WHP in Harrisburg. WHP had to go off the air to allow the Police station on. Colonel Stackpole, the treasurer argues this with the Radio Commission, the predecessor of the Federal Communications Commission. He characterizes it as a menace to freedom. He calls the State Police station the European System where the government controls the stations. He calls WHP the American System. I am darned sure he was correct. But the left leaning press today is really an arm of the Democrat party. It is worse then

---

WHP BATTLES FOR FREEDOM OF AIR AND THE PRESS

WBAK Interferes With Private Initiative, Radio Commission Told

By Associated Press

Washington, June 15.—The assertion that operation by the State of broadcasting station WBAK, Harrisburg, carrying with it the dangerous power of censorship, is a menace to freedom of the press and of the air was made today by Colonel E. J. Stackpole, Jr., treasurer of station WHP, Harrisburg, at a Radio Commission hearing.

WHP, operated by the Harrisburg Telegraph and sharing time on a wave length with WBAK, has asked the Commission for full time on the wave length. WBAK seeks renewal of its license on the same frequency.

Interferes With Private Initiative

"We contend that WHP typifies the American theory of broadcasting, while WBAK represents the government-operated European system," Colonel Stackpole said. "WBAK is a government-owned station," he added, "operating on a commercial frequency and interfering with private initiative, serving only a fraction of the peo-

(Continued on Page 13)

government control, it is control by one political party. In that it is far more dangerous. This will be discussed in detail later.

Unholy Alliances

When we see the term, 'alliances' we think of the formal interlocking non-aggression pacts that brought us World War I.   But there are many others, mostly not formal, sometimes even by enemies who have the same goal and seem to work together to attain it. One of those alliances in the 1960's was Hollywood and the ACLU. Hollywood wanted a more permissive society where, as the song says, "anything goes." They knew sex and violence would sell and more sex and violence would sell even more. Let me be honest, it sells because we will buy it. Hollywood pushed the envelope, the ACLU defended them on the 'free speech' doctrine and today, "anything goes," well at least if you are in the ACLU list of protected species. If you are a rapper, a protected species, you can use words and phrases even worse than the ones that got Imus taken off the air (who I thought should have been taken off the air just because he wasn't funny), you can use the 'N' word six times in a phrase, call women all kinds of nasty things or even advocate shooting police and that is 'protected expression.' Where did these lawyers who defend this garbage check their brains? Of course, if a white guy who is not in the elite or protected group does one of these, he will get a visit from the thought police, or be dragged through the national press. His employer will throw him under the bus.

The framers of the constitution intended that we should not be harassed for speaking our mind but if you look at that language it includes the right to redress and freedom of the press. I believe the center of that thrust was to not allow the government to restrict criticism. In that context freedom of speech is absolutely necessary for a society to be free. Oppressive governments absolutely need to keep dissent suppressed. Corollary to that is getting the tainted government message to the masses. I have sincere doubts that the framers of the constitution would have considered the filthy speech that is used and called art would have been included were they able to view it. I also look at any time the government inserts its will on free speech as a threat to it. Ironically, Colonel E. J. Stackpole Jr. made such a plea to the Radio Commission (the forerunner to the FCC) as recorded in the

Harrisburg Telegraph on June 15, 1932. He called the operation of a PA State police station (WBAK) a representation of the European Government System. The state police radio was on the same frequency (wavelength) and WHP was forced off the air for several hours a day while WBAK transmitted. In Europe in that era, the governments ran the radio stations. Radio was new, it was the hot product. People listened. And when the government ran the stations the people were fed the government's propaganda line. See the article in the previous section. Some of what happened in Europe in that era was exacerbated by the government media control. In Germany, the government controlled the radio broadcasting. Germany had a national network and Hitler had access to it. People were forbidden to listen to radio from outside such as BBC. The Colonel had it right then and his message is still valid today. With the left leaning news outlets and the radical left ideas of many in Hollywood we have today the equivalent of the state-run radio.

'Net neutrality' sounds like a great thing, but it puts government in control of the internet. I look back at the 'fairness doctrine' in broadcasting which was where the government decided what was fair and the damage to freedom it did. We must keep the government out of broadcasting (think no government finding for PBS too) and the internet. The proponents of net neutrality point out that without it, big business will have control of the internet. Yes. They will. But the alternative is big government. Five years ago, I trusted big business more than government. That was before the FBI and Justice Department used a dossier of lies to get a FISA warrant to spy on Americans. The best evidence today indicates the FISA judges at worst didn't ask questions but on the other hand the lawyers who presented it lied to the court. Part of any presentation like this should have included a disclaimer that the dossier was not confirmed and that it was paid for by a political campaign for the other candidate. I have asked myself, "if I were on that court and was told the dossier was prepared for and paid for by the Trump campaign, would I have been willing to order wiretaps on the Clinton campaign without supporting evidence?" I am darned sure I would have denied the warrant. I would have told them to come back when they had something valid to present. And I think the FISA would have handled that properly, had they known. There is an old statement that I only trust the guy as far as I can throw him. I only trust the government as far as I can throw it. As it gets bigger my 'throw distance' decreases. It is one of two reasons I object to government growth. The other is cost.

The overly violent movies and video games are another place this has been perverted. These have come to the point that they are desensitizing at least our kids and most likely all of us to violence. When you get killed in a video game you press the reset and you are back. Something about that concerns me. When we look at the rates of suicide, murder, drug abuse and domestic violence I get concerned that these games and movies are at least a small part of the problem, at least they are taking a person with a problem and making it worse. Black Panther, the much-touted and money maker movie has 169 violent killings in 135 minutes. That is one every 47 seconds.

I thought I was alone in this till a few days ago. I learned that every Surgeon General of the US with support of the medical and psychological groups have issued warnings about this. But nobody listens to reason. When the California passed a law to restrict the sale of these video games to minors it was contested in the court and it went to the Supreme Court where on a 7-2 decision the law was ruled unconstitutional on the grounds it limited free speech. No kidding, Calimexico passed such a law. That shows far more common sense than I thought existed in that whole state.

As far as I can determine the Surgeon Generals' warnings were never considered by the court but a poll of about 300 college professors who taught media subjects, and probably had no more psychology training that I have, maybe less, was presented. They were nearly unanimous in saying these games were not a problem. These are biased. They might as well polled 300 people who produce the games. An unholy alliance of Hollywood, college professors and the ACLU came together to defeat a law that may have saved lives! The individuals in the entertainment industry spout all kinds of things about how we should live, but they don't care about them or lives as long as the bucks continue to come in. I know I am broad brushing Hollywood and I am totally aware and want to make it clear, although that portion of the society that includes the

US entertainment industry is generally corrupt, I am like the scripture in Revelation 3:4.

> Thou hast a few names even in Sardis which have
> not defiled their garments; and they shall walk
> with me in white: for they are worthy.

Sardis was a terribly corrupt society, but the Apostle John says there are some there who have stayed honest. I am sure there are none anywhere who have not erred but there are some in the entertainment business, both historically like Eddie Cantor, who's name easily comes to mind, and more than a few today, mostly in the Country Music, who have tried to walk a straight path. Yes, they sometimes make a misstep and the press is on them like flies on honey. There are even some outside the Country venue that walk straight. Compare the music, presentation, and message from Seline Dijon, Ann Murray, and historic ones like the Carpenters, Bobby Vinton, Paul Anka, The Seekers, with that of some of the others who are not selling music, they are selling sex and violence, good examples being Lady Gaga and the hard-core rappers. Show me something good and wholesome in this trash and it will be the first I have seen.

At times I even wonder, can a Supreme Court Justice be rented? When a Harvey Weinstein can give hundreds of thousands of dollars to buy off a sexual encounter, why not a couple million for a couple votes on the supreme court to allow a market worth billions? Call it a small investment. There are a couple idiots on the court who will vote the sex and violence line. At a million each, it only takes a couple million to swing a vote since many decisions are 5 to 4. Does it matter if it is illegal? Would the entertainment industry do something illegal? Some of them have already answered that when they had the illegal encounter with the woman. So what? The justification is simple, "Everyone is doing it."

I will relate a personal item here. Our work group was walking back from a meeting. It was during the Bill Clinton and Monica Lewinski mess. One of the guys mentioned it and commented it was terrible. A guy in the group, a 40 plus year old with a wife and a couple kids said, "What is the big deal about it? Everyone does it."

I was pissed with the comment. I have never done it. I have had sex with one woman in my life, the woman I was married to for 40 years and all those encounters were after 2 PM on August 6, 1967. Everyone does not do it. I responded to him, "If you say that again, modify it to, everyone but Ralph is doing it. I am not. I hear it again I am going to get a lawyer and see if I can sue for slander."

He spluttered. One of the other guys chimed in, "Include me on that. I am not." That was followed by about 5 more who said the same thing. I am pretty sure none of them were. At the worst, if they had done it, they saw it as wrong.

Sometime later he was given the option of being fired or resign because he was having sex with a 19 year old intern. "Everyone was doing it" was a self-justification for his indiscretion. Everyone is not doing it. No. Not everyone is doing it. Let's see. Slick Willie was doing that and didn't get fired. Left leaning politics has a lower standard than business.

One of the strangest sets of bedfellows are the radical left and the extreme Muslims. Let's face it, the Antifa and their fellow travelers including Occupy, Black Lives Matter, and some other lefties are working with Muslims to destroy freedom in this country. As an aside, BLM could entice me to join their struggle if they replaced Black with All. Black makes it racist, all makes it inclusive.

How someone on the radical right can support the efforts of those on the radical left and vice versa is beyond me. Let it be clear, Moderate Muslims are to the right of the Tea Party! Radical Muslims are to the right of the Moderates. Politically there is a chasm between the left wing Antifa and right-wing Radical Islam unless somewhere out there we have a channel that connects them. I believe that channel exists, it is a channel of hate, disruption and most important, ego, and greed. For the Muslim it is a hatred for anything non-Muslim. It is an ego that only they know what is right. It is a greed that they must control the world under Islam. They are trying to please a god that is an invention of the sick and twisted mind of Mohammed. The gods of the Greeks and Romans make more sense. If you read the Koran, you will see a religion of hatred. One of the big differences between Christianity and Islam other than Christianity embraces Christ as savior and the Son of

God while Islam calls him a prophet and denies he is the Son of God is the idea of revenge which is prohibited in Christianity and demanded in Islam. 'An eye for an eye' appears in the Koran and the Bible but it is a demanded for retribution in the Koran and is the limit of punishment in Judaism and that is before the cross. Even further under Christianity we are enjoined to not exact any revenge.

And the women's movement has thrown in on this and in the march after Trump's inauguration called for Sharia Law in the US. These feminists were there screaming for Sharia! Under it, a woman is no more than property, with no rights, and her testimony and value in inheritance is one half of a man. She inherits one half of what her brother does and if it takes the testimony of two men to convict a man of a crime, it takes the testimony of four women!

Allow me to delve into a little theology. The denial of Christ being the Son of God is based on a misunderstanding of God and mono-theism – the concept of one god – just one of Mohammed's many misunderstandings. Mohammed called Christianity polytheism – more than one god – because Mohammed did not understand the trinity, Father, Son and Holy Spirit. He called it polytheism. It is not. Jesus said, "The Father and I are one." The Father, Son and Holy Spirit do not work separately. They are one. Mohammed called Jesus a prophet, but not the Son of God. Jesus said he was the Son of God. Either He is the Son of God and Mohammed is wrong or he is not the son of God and Mohammed has recognized Jesus, who he calls a liar, as a prophet. Mo can't have it both ways.

A second difference is in what is called evangelism. Mohammed allowed and even encouraged forced conversions, i.e. conversions to Islam on threat of death. People were and still are being killed to convert or being killed if they leave Islam. The death threat was and to this day is real. The true teaching of Christianity has never allowed this and although a few sects of it have done some despicable things, they were not following the teaching of Christ. The teaching is clear, "It is the goodness of God that leads men to repentance." The Crusades and the excesses of the "church" during the dark ages were never in line with the teaching of Christ. Let's face it, the Crusades were a whipped up concept, not a Godly one. The "church" in the dark ages was not by any standard carrying out the teachings of Jesus. The world went into the dark ages because the light of God went out in the church. That light returned with the Protestant Reformation and the world followed the church into the light.

Even the Muslim confession, "There is one God, Allah and Mohammed is his prophet" would have been rejected by the Apostle Paul who wrote:

> 1 Corinthians 1:12 Now this I say, that every one of you saith, I am of Paul; and I of Apollos; and I of Cephas; and I of Christ.

Paul rejected the very thing that Muslims are doing with Mohammed, having people revere, or more correctly worship a man. They will kill over a cartoon. Mohammed's 'honor' is more important than human life. Both Islam and Christianity have the theme, "Thou shalt have no other gods before me." Muslims are taught to violate that every day. But then, Jesus, Paul and other bible writers have warned us against false prophets. Mohammed is one of them, with his being wrong on some things, how can we assume he is not on others? Let us face it, Islam is a perversion of Christianity.

For the radical left it is a hatred for anything they disagree with. They are no less dogmatic than the Radical Muslim. There is no room for any bending, for accepting any other view. It is an ego that they know what is best for the rest of us. They will disrupt life for many with their demonstrations that all too often turn to looting and burning, risk lives, and shout down a speaker. It is a greed that others have what they want and it does not matter if they are lazy, broke and living in their parents basement or millionaires on Wall Street. They want what is yours. They will take it in any way they can.

These two forces are working at destroying the foundations of this nation. Both hate Judeo-Christian values. They work at every corner to tear them down. They consider the ten commandments a threat and after all they are to a perverted and disobedient lifestyle. Those commandments say we should not lie, steal, murder, covet what is our neighbor's, or commit adultery.

The Muslims see a free society as wrong, all must be subjugated to Islam. They fail to see God wants a person to willingly love Him, not be forced to by threats of violence. It is the basic attribute of God that Mohammed missed in his quest.

The left sees the constitution as a restraint on their agenda, they have since at least FDR who wanted to pack the supreme court, discussed elsewhere in this writing. Both of these entities erode our society with any means they can find.

The left sees the family as a problem. They have pressed for free love which resulted in massive numbers of teen pregnancies, abortion that kills 20% of our children in utero, government oversight of the family on the idea that a bureaucrat in DC knows better what is best for our kids, and a welfare system that puts fathers out of the home. The government should provide a support system for the family. When a manufacturing process is flawed, the product it produces is flawed. The left has introduced things into the school, home and family that have flawed the process of raising children, and all too often the product turns out to be an adult that is not a benefit to either themselves or society. They are so filled with fear, shame, greed and hate that they are willing to kill to make a statement or get a fix. Teaching the left-wing line, the perversions, the hate, the division is more important than math, science, history or language, unless it can be perverted to include their lines. We no longer teach history. We teach it as the liberals want it to have been. We no longer teach language. It is oriented to promoting leftist dogma.

Islam does not see the family as does Christian teaching. They talk a good talk, but it is more in line with the extreme Puritan teaching with the backdrop of violence. To a Muslim, the wife is not a partner. She is a possession like a cow, a car or a house, to be used, abused if it suits his fancy, and discarded if it does not satisfy him. The Apostle Paul tells the Christian man, "Husbands love your wife as Christ loved the church and gave his life for it." Christ loved the church enough to allow the unholy alliance of the Romans and the Jewish leaders to hang him on a cross. He gave his life for the church. A husband should give his life for his wife. At one time I looked at that and asked, "how?" As I spent years with my wife, I learned that giving one's life does not necessarily mean the literal death. It means giving of your life daily for that person, to meet their needs, financial, mental, physical and emotional. I can attest that when a woman's needs are met, the guy finds a life of joy. Nearly eleven years after her death she still 'lights up my life.' It is interesting that the passage I quoted above, 'husbands love your wives…' is by the same writer, the Apostle Paul who is vilified by the 'women's movement' as a woman hater.

Allow me to show that in another setting. The Battle Hymn of the Republic has a line, "As he died to make men holy, let us <u>die</u> to make men free." Anita Bryant who was the first person to sing that publicly in the south changed the line to, "As he died to make men holy, let us <u>live</u> to make men free." The first time I heard that I felt she was wrong in the change and then I started to see it. If we <u>live</u> to make men free, to help free them from bondages of any kind, to protect them from harm and evil, we will have to <u>die</u>, at least to our selfish desires and maybe even give up life itself. Whether the word in that line is live or die is irrelevant. If we have honor, it is what we do. We may not be called as the men in blue in that struggle, to hold Little Round Top or Culps Hill[97] in peril of death, but we are called to lay down thoughts, ideas, and <u>prejudices</u>, put aside pleasures, give of our finances, self and time to make men free. "As he died to make men holy, let us both live and die to make men free." We need to do whatever it takes. It is unlikely but possible that we could be called to make what is called the ultimate sacrifice to do this but no matter what, we are called to live for our fellow man.

---

[97] Little Round Top and Culps Hill were the two ends of the Union line at Gettysburg. They were held on the second and third days of the battle by men, many of whom gave their lives to keep those out of rebel hands. Had either fell, and the rebels pressed them hard, within a few hours the Confederates would have placed cannon here and the Union line would almost certainly have been untenable and had to be abandoned. With those remaining in Union hands the rebels chose to cross the fields in the devastating assault called Pickets Charge. Although there were Union losses in repelling this attack, about 1500, they were small compared to the losses of the rebels. Of the 12,500 men who started across that field, nearly half were casualties, killed or wounded and many were captured. Lee lost about 25,000 of his 75,000 men in the three days. The union losses were about 23,000 of about 104,000.

The Wolf Plan

On March 13, 2020 Pennsylvania Governor Tom Wolf announced a move to contain the COVID-19 virus. Over the last 4 months he has raped the state economy with restrictions. The basis for these restrictions were hidden. The method of getting an exemption to open a business was hidden. The job of determining who got exemptions was handed to the Department of Community and Economic Development, the one that has made one bad decision after another on development. I could understand the process not being made public at the time but now four months later, the governor has vowed to veto a bill that will require more transparency. It would open these records! If what he and his political shills did was righteous, why hide it? Why not show it to the state as an example of how good a job he has done. The bill did pass and became law without his signature. It passed unanimously in senate. An override of his veto was a near certainty. He allowed it to become law.

His first decision was to close the state for two weeks, probably the best decision he made but really? Essential workers were still out there and with very little direction on safety. The federal government was issuing guidelines but Wolf, a committed Democrat Leftist decided that anything Republican wasn't worth listening to. Face it, the information from the feds wasn't great but it was based on the best information we had at that time and the team of Trump put together was awesome. They bickered, they disagreed at times, they even at times disagreed with Trump which in any other situation would have gotten, "You're fired." Trump was smart enough to realize that the best experts would at times disagree! Wolf put together a team, him and the Secretary of Health. What a brain trust to manage a state of 12.8 million people. A left wing socialist and a discredited, mixed up, psychologist! Maybe he should have looked for a medical doctor who finished last in his class? But when the appointment was made, he chose a psychologist whose main selling point was, she is the ugliest woman in Pennsylvania. I have been told she is transgender. That and her being ugly aren't important to me. That she lacks solid medical credentials does. Worse, she and Wolf decided to not agree to follow CDC guidelines. That is akin to a mechanic telling his lawyer, you don't know what you are doing when it comes to legal matters. Sure, the CDC didn't have it down perfect, but nobody did.

Wolf had COVID positive nursing home patients moved to other nursing homes, probably not a bad idea in itself but this was hidden from the public, maybe defensible, but he also hid it from the local officials! That only was discovered in June when one county commissioner in a meeting with the commissioner from another county said, "You got our COVID positive patients." The commissioner didn't just go on this, he found one of the patients, called him and asked what he could see out of his window. The guy was in his county!

If you are going to place your positive patients in one place it is incumbent on you to make that action safe for the patients and community and that means, letting at least the leaders of that county know. Wolf failed here in a basic task. The Secretary of Health moved her mom out of a nursing home!

As mentioned before the setting of exemptions was masked in secrecy. I personally believe, based on businesses that were allowed to open that were like ones that were not, politics played a role. I base that on two things. First, I worked with most Commonwealth agencies for 13 years. I saw the good and bad. If I were to classify the agencies at that time, Aging and SERS would have been my picks of most efficient and ethical. The other end of the spectrum would have been Pennsylvania Commission on Crime and Delinquency (PCCD), the Liquor Control Board (LCB), the Gaming Control Board a.k.a. the Governor's Corruption Board (GCB), followed in last place by Department of Community and Economic Development (DCED). A side note, I called PDE the largest collection of drones and misfits I have ever seen. I saw people there working harder to get out of work than doing it. I will add, more than 80 percent of the people there are doing a job, doing it well, often in spite of the leadership. Remember, most "Secretaries of" didn't get their job because they were capable, they got them because they were political hacks. The level below them is usually as bad. What I saw of some of the most maligned agencies was far better than their outside reputation. It will surprise many that I rate PENDOT in the next three under SERS. I put the LCB where I do, based on some shady practices I saw first-hand. Remember, they regulate themselves! The GCB under

Rendell put their own team together to investigate the potential license holders, mostly political hacks, and ignored a good investigative team, PSP. The only rationale, Rendell could dictate what the political hacks could do, but not PSP. His rejection of PSP put them up one notch for me.

So why the problem with DCED? Easy. They were the only agency who asked me to do something unethical, then threatened me if I did not. Fortunately, my boss ignored the threat. When I learned DCED was doing the exemptions I laughed and said, "Hope someone who is applying for one has a record of good contributions to the Wolf or Democrat campaigns." The scripture says what is done in secret is evil and Wolf has worked to keep it hidden.

What would have worked? Set some guidelines, social distancing, disinfecting, etc. Tell business you need to meet these to open, not some tainted bureaucrat telling who can.

But the plan was simple. Kill the economy. Why? For the worst reason Wolf put Pennsylvania through hell. To have a bad economy in November to beat Trump!

Then we started opening. There were the red, yellow, green phases with no public disclosure on how that decision would be made. Again, there was partiality and even now millions of dollars are being withheld from Lebanon County because the county commissioners grew some backbone and told Wolf, "No." What is done in secret.

A bill was put on his desk altering the emergency powers, he vetoed it. A second bill now, asking for transparency is on his desk, unanimous passage in the legislature. He is going to veto it! (He let is become law without his signature.) This is how to piss off the legislature. In York County we were under illegal house arrest till the end of June.

There was no common sense approach, just the Whim of Wolf.

Conclusion

When writing this I got to this point and asked, "How do I frame the conclusions?" I got that answer on November 22, 2017 when I heard

George Washington's Thanksgiving message being read. I feel it must be included here as it shows the framework for what I see.

Thanksgiving Proclamation

[New York, 3 October 1789]

By the President of the United States of America. a Proclamation.

Whereas it is the duty of all Nations to acknowledge the providence of Almighty God, to obey his will, to be grateful for his benefits, and humbly to implore his protection and favor—and whereas both Houses of Congress have by their joint Committee requested me "to recommend to the People of the United States a day of public thanksgiving and prayer to be observed by acknowledging with grateful hearts the many signal favors of Almighty God especially by affording them an opportunity peaceably to establish a form of government for their safety and happiness."

Now therefore I do recommend and assign Thursday the 26th day of November next to be devoted by the People of these States to the service of that great and glorious Being, who is the beneficent Author of all the good that was, that is, or that will be—That we may then all unite in rendering unto him our sincere and humble thanks—for his kind care and protection of the People of this Country previous to their becoming a Nation—for the signal and manifold mercies, and the favorable interpositions of his Providence which we experienced in the course and conclusion of the late war—for the great degree of tranquillity, union, and plenty, which we have since enjoyed—for the peaceable and rational manner, in which we have been enabled to establish constitutions of government for our safety and happiness, and particularly the national One now lately instituted—for the civil and religious liberty with which we are blessed; and the means we have of acquiring and diffusing useful knowledge; and in general for all the great and various favors which he hath been pleased to confer upon us.

and also that we may then unite in most humbly offering our prayers and supplications to the great Lord and Ruler of Nations and beseech him to pardon our national and other transgressions—to enable us all, whether in public or private stations, to perform our several and relative duties properly and punctually—to render our national government a blessing to all the people, by constantly being a Government of wise, just, and constitutional laws, discreetly and faithfully executed and obeyed—to protect and guide all Sovereigns and Nations (especially such as have shewn kindness unto us) and to bless them with good government, peace, and concord—To promote the knowledge and practice of true religion and virtue, and the encrease of science among them and us—and generally to grant unto all Mankind such a degree of temporal prosperity as he alone knows to be best.

Given under my hand at the City of New-York the third day of October in the year of our Lord 1789.[98]

I find the anthesis of oppression in the President's words, with special attention to these points.

"..and also that we may then unite in most humbly offering our prayers and supplications to the great Lord and Ruler of Nations and beseech him to pardon our national and other transgressions—to enable us all, whether in public or private stations, to perform our several and relative duties properly and punctually—to render our national government a blessing to all the people, by constantly being a Government of wise, just, and constitutional laws, discreetly and faithfully executed and obeyed—to protect and guide all Sovereigns and Nations (especially such as have shewn kindness unto us) and to bless them with good government, peace, and concord—"

I find the section, *'most humbly offering our prayers and supplications to the great Lord and Ruler of Nations and beseech him to pardon our national and other transgressions'* so filled with wisdom. Our country, although far from perfection has done well in many of its actions. At times they were not without some travail, the ending of slavery, the right to vote for women, the integration of schools, to mention a few but we came through them and are better for it. We need to ask God and our brothers and sisters for pardon for our transgressions. This goes far beyond the black slavery issue which we must certainly do, not personally, not hold as a sin, but we need to be sensitive to our brothers and sisters of all colors with the understanding that we know this existed, it was evil and we will work to avoid a repeat of such on either a macro or micro level. I have already discussed that there needs to be forgiveness and walking away from that in the black community. It needs to include the Japanese who were relocated, the Indians for the trail of Tears, the immigrants who were abused, all of them, including Slavs, Irish, Chinese, and yes, even the Germans and Italians. Every group has faced some of this. It comes also to the so-called little things we fail in daily. The Lord's prayer includes, "Forgive us out trespasses." I too often have to mention to ones around me, "I am sorry. I screwed up." The scripture notes, "forgive and you shall be forgiven."[99] Many in

---

[98] https://founders.archives.gov/documents/Washington/05-04-02-0091

our society who feel they have been wronged, no matter if the wrong is real, partially real or imagined will only be free when they forgive. They are in a self-induced bondage. And just as important, it is well to remember these abuses to prevent us doing other despicable things but to continually beat people for what happened years ago is not productive.

As a Christian counselor who has walked people through being liberated from their pasts, personal, family and societal, and one who personally has shucked much of this and still has a way to go, I can attest that until you forgive others, forgive yourself in how you have taken on the hatred and hurt and then forgive God for where you have held Him responsible for what happened, you will be in bondage. You will be tied to that person or group who in your mind wronged you until you break that chain. Note I said, "who in your mind wronged you." Whether the wrong is real or imagined, it holds you in bondage. Like Ber Rabbit, you will be stuck to the tar baby of the ought you hold against your brothers and sisters and quite frankly it is a self-curse that could even be a factor to shorten your life. I can guarantee it will reduce the quality of that life. Forgiveness is a mandatory thing and as I watch the current leaders of various movements, I see nothing but bile and hatred. By the words of their mouths they are condemned.[100] They are stuck to the tar baby and are holding others to it by the tar of their words.

The alt-left is working hard to create more victims by declaring people victims, by pointing out offensives, real, imagined and cooked up.

The oppression can stop but it is up to us. We will either go to the polls and elect better men and women, hold them to the right way or we will continue to live in the oppression. We can either throw out those who would oppress us or we will live in tyranny.

As Ellie Johnson a fictional character in one of my novels, "The First Family" said. "I want to be free. Will you walk with me to freedom?"[101]

---

[99] Luke_6:37 Judge not, and you shall not be judged. Condemn not, and you shall not be condemned. Forgive, and you shall be forgiven.
[100] Matthew 12:37 For by your words you shall be justified, and by your words you shall be condemned.
[101] Attack on the First Family.

The way to that freedom is love and respect for one another and rejecting the swan songs of the politicians who will enslave us with promises of handouts and the charlatans who would enslave us by hawking their hatreds. They exist on all portions of the political spectrum and in every ethnic group. The government handouts of today as prescribed by the socialists are the trail of breadcrumbs that lead us into the trap of oppression.

My prayer is may you forgive, stand strong, fight the good fight. "A good fight is the fight you win."[102]

I love the passage in Galatians 5:1, "Stand fast therefore in the liberty wherewith Christ hath made us free, and be not entangled again with the yoke of bondage." (KJV) It is a fantastic verse about the liberty that Christ paid for by his death on the cross, his resurrection and ascension. But there is a corollary for the American. I will take some liberty and use this scripture as a model. "Stand fast therefore in the liberty wherewith the Constitution of the Unites States has made us free and be not entangled again with the yoke of bondage imposed by an oppressive government in allowing our freedoms to be eroded for a bowl of pottage, security and a handout." The apostle Paul writes, "Having done all to stand, stand..." I can only echo that in both settings.

Ralph Brandt

Placed here for E-Book readers

Ralph Brandt was born in a row home in Hunters Run Pennsylvania. He graduated from Shippensburg State College with a BA Mathematics but had a love for World War and Civil War History. He works with an overall subject but brings it down to the people and what is happening to them. Currently he has 21 novels and 4 historical studies. Amassing Power started as a comment in a novel and became a serious study. He researches from period literature, not the modern, regurgitated pablum.

---

[102] From the song, "It is Written" by David Elgels.

Oppression has been with us in various forms since the beginning of time. The feudal system, the brutal governments, the Inquisition, both sides of the Crusades, Communism, Nazism, show it can come from any quarter. This study starts as America was facing the most devastating war in its history, The War of Southern Rebellion, incorrectly called the Civil War. This war ultimately ended slavery, one form of oppression, but prosecuting it brought more oppression and the backwash of it opened the door for a revival of oppression, the neo-slavery of Government oppression. This war extended beyond the battle fields, past 1865, when it extended into the hearts of men and the Bible says those are intensely wicked. That wickedness reared its ugly head about 1895 and continued till well into the 20th Century with hellish practices that were in too many cases, not infractions of the law, but provided by the law itself. Some of that evil continues to drive actions to this day. This is an abridged study, a complete one is beyond this author. I believe that in pointing out the ones I have, the astute reader will be able to ferret out others.